THE ETERNAL HERMES

By the same author

Les Vampires (Essai historique, critique et littéraire)
Paris: Le Terrain Vague, 1962

Kirchberger et l'Illuminisme du dix-huitième siècle
The Hague: Martinus Nijhoff, 1966

Eckartshausen et la théosophie chrétienne
Paris: Klincksieck, 1969

L'Esotérisme au XVIIIè siècle en France et en Allemagne
Paris: Seghers-Laffont, 1973

Mystiques, théosophes et Illuminés au siècle des Lumières
Hildesheim: G. Olms, 1977

Les Contes de Grimm (Mythe et Initiation)
Paris: Les Lettres Modernes, 1978

Access to Western Esotericism
Albany: State University of New York Press, 1994

The Golden Fleece and Alchemy
Albany: State University of New York Press, 1993

Philosophie de la Nature (Physique Sacrée—Théosophie)
Paris: Albin Michel, 1995

THE ETERNAL HERMES

From Greek God to Alchemical Magus

With thirty-nine plates

Antoine Faivre

Translated by
Joscelyn Godwin

PHANES PRESS

Book and cover design by David Fideler.

Phanes Press publishes many fine books on the philosophical, spiritual, and cosmological traditions of the Western world. To receive a complete catalogue, please write:

Phanes Press, PO Box 6114, Grand Rapids, MI 49516, USA.

Library of Congress Cataloging-in-Publication Data

Faivre, Antoine, 1934–
    The eternal Hermes : from Greek god to alchemical magus / Antoine Faivre ; translated by Joscelyn Godwin
      p. cm.
    Articles originally in French, published separately.
    Includes bibliographical references and index.
    ISBN 0-933999-53-4 (alk. paper) — ISBN 0-933999-52-6
(pbk. : alk. paper)
    1. Hermes (Greek deity) 2. Hermes, Trismegistus. 3. Hermetism—
History. 4. Alchemy—History. I. Title
BL920.M5F35   1995
135'.4—dc20   95-3854
                                                   CIP

Printed on permanent, acid-free paper.

Printed in the United States of America.

Contents

Chapter Four

Chapter Five

Chapter Six

For Lionel Robbe-Jedeau

PREFACE

The title of this collection encompasses two figures who are both distinct and complementary: Hermes-Mercurius, the God with the caduceus, who belongs to Greek and Roman mythology, and Hermes Trismegistus, whose appearance can be traced back to the early Alexandian epoch. Each of the six chapters stands on its own, having been published separately, and deals either with the God Hermes, or with Hermes Trismegistus—or with both. Given the similar inspiration running through all six essays, David Fideler and Joscelyn Godwin suggested that they might constitute an anthology endowed with some homogeneity. Therefore, for the purpose of the present edition, the articles in this volume have been for the most part corrected and enlarged, and their inevitable overlappings have been reduced. In their original version, they were published as follows:

Chapter 1: "Hermès," in *Dictionnaire des mythes littéraires*, ed. Pierre Brunel (Paris: Editions du Rocher, 1988), pp.705–732.

Chapter 2: "The Children of Hermes and the Science of Man," published in English in *Hermeticism in the Renaissance (Intellectual History and the Occult in Early Modern Europe)*, ed. Ingrid Merkel and Allen G. Debus (Washington: The Folger Shakespeare Library; London and Toronto: Associated Presses, 1988), pp.24–48. From Symposium held in March, 1982, at the Institute for Renaissance and Eighteenth Century Studies in the Folger Shakespeare Library, Washington, D.C.

Chapter 3: "D'Hermès-Mercure à Hermès Trismégiste: au confluent du mythe et du mythique," in *Présence d'Hermès Trismégiste*, ed. Antoine Faivre and Frédérick Tristan (Paris: Albin Michel, series "Cahiers de l'Hermétisme," 1988). From Symposium held in July, 1985, in Cerisy-La-Salle on "The Myth and the Mythical."

Chapter 4: "Présence d'Hermès dans la ville (Le *Picatrix*, Gustav Meyrink, Luis Buñuel, George Miller)," in *O Imaginário da*

11

Cidáde, ed. Yvette K. Centeno (Lisbon: Calouste Gulbenkian Foundation, Acardte, 1989), pp.337–349. From Symposium held in October, 1985, in Lisbon on "The Imaginary of the Town."

Chapter 5: "Visages d'Hermès Trismégiste," in *Présence d'Hermès Trismégiste* [see above], pp.49–99.

Chapter 6: "La postérité de l'hermétisme alexandrin: repères historiques et bibliographiques," in *Présence d'Hermès Trismégiste* [see above], pp.13–23.

I offer my personal thanks to Joscelyn Godwin, not only for translating the entire volume, but also for enriching it with new references. My thanks also goes to David Fideler for his editorial counsel, and to Jean-Pierre Mahé for completing my information on some particular aspects of the Hermetica.

—ANTOINE FAIVRE

CHAPTER ONE

Hermes in the Western Imagination

Introduction: The Greek Hermes

Just as the daylight penetrates at dawn through every crack and crevice, says the author of the Homeric Hymn, so Hermes slipped silently in through the keyhole of the cavern which gave him birth. How plastic, mobile, and ambiguous is the nature of this god, whose feminine companions are Hermione, Harmonia, and above all Iris, who precedes him with breezy feet and wings of gold! In Greek mythology, Hermes appears as an engaging and complex figure, in forms both mobile and definitive, so that one must first know these myths in order to follow his tracks through the long path of the Western imagination, from the Middle Ages to the present. They are the essential reference, like the omnipresent background of a picture: so familiar, or at least so accessible to us that there is no need here to retell the stories in which Greek Hermes, or Latin Mercury, plays the protagonist, the hero, or a walk-on role. We will just recall some of his characteristics that have been constantly repeated and emphasized from Antiquity to modern times.

Two of these traits stand out from the tangled undergrowth: first, his guiding function, linked to his extreme mobility; second, his mastery of speech and interpretation, warrant of a certain type of knowledge. Virgil, well aware of Mercury's plasticity, describes how the lively messenger of the gods controls wind and clouds with his magic wand, flying through them like a bird. But this traveler does not follow strict or planned itineraries: as Karl Kerényi suggests, he is more of a "journeyer" than a "traveler." Just as the geographical goal of a honeymoon is of little importance, so Mercury wanders about and communicates for the sheer pleasure of it. His route is not the shortest distance between two points: it

is a world in itself, made of serpentine paths where chance and the
unforeseen may happen. *Hermaion* means "fallen fruit" or "wind-
fall." To profit from windfalls does not exclude the possibility of
giving destiny a slight nudge, through tricks and subterfuges. Thus
one sometimes finds Hermes unearthing hidden treasures; and it is
only a short step from there to making off with them! "Hermes
[*Hermaion*] in common!" said the Greeks on making a lucky find,
just as one says in English "Equal shares all round!" In the same
spirit, eclecticism is justified—and plagiarism, too; but "stealing"
is not a good rendering of the Greek *kleptein*, which suggests rather
the idea of a ruse, in the sense of a "secret action." (Compare the
German word *Täuschung*, and the charming verb *verschalken*.)
And is not hermeneutics all about bringing hidden treasures to
light?

Hermes, unlike Prometheus, steals things only in order to put
them back into circulation. Thus one could speak of his function
as psychopomp as encompassing the "circulation" of souls. This
function is dual, for Hermes is not content merely to lead souls to
the kingdom of the dead: he also goes there to find them and bring
them back to the land of the living (cf. *Aeneid* IV, 242, and many
examples from the Middle Ages up to modern times). Through all
his varied representations in folklore, art, and literature, the Western imagination has always stressed this relational aspect of Hermes,
which is the common denominator of attributes that range from
the transition of souls to thievery, also touching on commerce,
magic, poetry, and learning.

Athenaeus and others ascribe to Hermes the glory of discovering
the arts and sciences, while the Homeric Hymn (verses 25ff.) makes
him the inventor of the seven-stringed lyre. He is the master of
knowledge, or rather of a means of attaining to a knowledge that
may be gnostic, eclectic, or transdisciplinary—or all of these at
once. Perhaps he is largely indebted to Plato for this. Not long after
the *Plutus* of Aristophanes, where Hermes appears in a comic role,
Plato's *Cratylus* derives his name from the Greek word for an
interpreter: "I should imagine that the name Hermes has to do with

speech, and signifies that he is the interpreter, or messenger, or thief, or liar, or bargainer; all that sort of thing has a great deal to do with language" (*Cratylus* 408A, Jowett translation). This is the only aspect retained by the New Testament, in Acts 14, where the inhabitants of Lystra take Paul for Hermes because they find him a master of words. Thus poets and philosophers also revere him. Virgil's contemporary Horace places himself under the special protection of Mercury. Lucian, in *Fugitivi* (XXII), shows Hermes accompanying Heracles and Philosophy in their pursuit of the Cynics, because Apollo says that it is Hermes who can best distinguish the true philosophers from the false ones. His is the role of the sage—even a facetious and playful one—rather than the hero: the trait emphasized by the *Iliad*. The world of that epic is definitely not that of Hermes, who does not even appear there to guide a soul, and keeps himself aloof from all heroic action. He opposes Leto, but dodges aside and will not face her. Zeus sends him to Priam, who wishes to get the body of his son back from Achilles; he is less a messenger than a guide, and it is he who prepares the escape by putting the guards to sleep. Wotan, who was already recognized by the Romans as comparable to Mercury (Tacitus, *Germ.* IX), also has characteristics of this kind. Furthermore, when this Germanic god finds himself in certain comical predicaments, we sense that Harlequin is not far away: the clown whose stick or wooden sword is nothing but a puny caduceus.

The Thrice-Greatest

Hermes-Mercury's plasticity allowed him to take on a special form at the beginning of our era, bringing out his most serious and least playful aspect. This was his manifestation as Hermes Trismegistus, which remains alive to this day. Two factors seem to have been involved in it. On the one hand, there was the allegorical interpretation of mythology that began with Homeric exegesis in the fourth century BCE, and tended increasingly towards euhemerism. (Euhemerus, third century BCE, saw the gods as actual human beings who were divinized after death.) This led to a belief in

Hermes as a historic person who had been divinized: a tendency reinforced by Christian thought, which was resolutely euhemerist from the second century onwards. The second factor was the attraction of Graeco-Roman paganism towards ancient Egypt: part of the need that the Greeks felt for exalting Barbarian philosophy to the detriment of their own. This attraction was reinforced by the existence of a Greek culture in Alexandria, firmly installed on Egyptian soil in the land of pyramids and hieroglyphs. Around the beginning of our era, the Greeks justifiably saw in Thoth the first figuration of Hermes, or even the same personage under a different name. Aided by the euhemerist tendency, Thoth-Mercury was credited with a great number of books—quite real ones—under the general title of *Hermetica*. Almost all of them were written in Greek, in the Nile Delta region, from just before the Christian Era until the third century; they treat astrology, alchemy, and theosophy. The most famous ones, from the second and third centuries CE, are grouped under the general title of the *Corpus Hermeticum*, in which the *Asclepius* and the Fragments collected by Stobaeus have been included. But a more fantastic tradition attributed thousands of other works to Hermes Trismegistus.

The twenty-third Fragment of Stobaeus describes the court of the Lord, the builder of the universe, as it existed before the presence of mortals. Hermes appears there as "soul" (*psyche*), possessing a bond of sympathy with the mysteries of Heaven; he is sent by God into our lower world in order to teach true knowledge. The Lord commands Hermes to participate in the creation of mankind as steward and administrator. Thus one can see him as the principal actor, after the supreme deity, in the anthropogonic drama. He is a soul that has descended here as the first divine emanation, preceding the second emanation represented by Isis and Osiris, who are also sent to this lower world for the instruction of humanity. Here Hermes is not styled Trismegistus ("Thrice-Greatest"), but the other texts of the *Corpus Hermeticum* more than suggest that it is he. This is one of the numerous examples of shifting or transition between the figure of the sage Trismegistus, who is a mortal, and the god of Olympus. At this epoch, we have not only a euhemeristic process, but also a reverse euhemerism: Hermes Trismegistus is both the precipitation of Mercury into human history and the sublimation of history to Olympus. These fluctuations, or rather this twofold motion, favors a fluid genealogy and the presence of several Hermeses.

The most classic genealogy, contrived in the Hellenistic era during the third or second century BCE, starts the Hermes series with Thoth, who carved his knowledge on stelae and concealed it. His son was Agathodemon, who himself begat the second Hermes, called Trismegistus, whose son was Tat. Apollonius Rhodius (*Argonautica* I, 640f.) tells us that Hermes, through his son Aithalides, was a direct ancestor of Pythagoras. But nothing is more uncertain than divine genealogies. According to the traditions presented by Plutarch, Isis was the daughter of Hermes; while Cicero (*De Natura Deorum* III, 22) counts no fewer than five Mercurys: the son of Heaven and Day; the son of Valens and the nymph Phoronis; the son of the Third Jupiter and Maia; the son of Nilus, whom the Egyptians will not name; and lastly "Theyt," who slew Argus, says Cicero, and taught the Egyptians laws and writing.

As for Saint Augustine, in the *City of God* he makes Trismegistus the great-grandson of a contemporary of Moses, and euhemerizes by regarding extraordinary human actions as the origin of Hermes and the other Greek gods. Isidore of Seville (sixth to seventh century), also a euhemerist, devotes many passages of his *Etymologiarum sive libri XX* to Hermes (e.g., VIII, XI, 1ff. XI. 45–49), seeing him as a pagan fiction based on the historical existence of a person who invented the lyre, the flute, conjuring and tricks ("*Praestigium vero Mercurius primus dicitur invenisse*"—"Mercury is said to have been the first inventor of illusions").

Although derivative from Isidore's *Etymologia*, the *Chronicle of the Six Ages of the World* of Adon of Vienne bears witness, like many other works, to the significant ambiguity of Hermes, as Mercury and/or Trismegistus. Adon writes: "It is said that in those times there lived Prometheus, who is supposed to have fashioned men out of mud. At the same time, his brother Atlas was considered a great astrologer. Atlas's grandson Mercury was a wise man, skilled in many arts, for which reason, after his death, the aberrations of his contemporaries placed him among the gods" (Migne, *Patrologiae Cursus, series Latina* CXXIII, col.35). Similarly, the *Book of Treasure* of Brunetto Latini numbers Mercury with Moses, Solon, Lycurgus, Numa Pompilius, and the Greek king Phoroneus, as the first law-givers to whom humanity is greatly indebted. Hermes-Mercury, in dual form, thus takes his place among the tutelary gods of civilization. Strabo says that he gave the Egyptians their laws and taught philosophy and astronomy to the priests of Thebes; Marcus Manilius goes so far as to see in him the founder of the Egyptian religion. For Jacopo of Bergamo, Minerva was the first woman to know the art of working wool, and Chiron the inventor of medicine; Hermes Trismegistus was the first astronomer, and Mercury the first musician, while Atlas taught astrology to the Greeks. There are similar attributions in Polydore Virgil: from Hermes, we learned the divisions of time, while Mercury taught the Egyptians the alphabet and knowledge of the stars.

The Arabic Idris and the Alchemical Mercury

The name of Hermes, whether or not qualified as Trismegistus, henceforth served as guarantee or signature for a host of esoteric books on magic, astrology, medicine, etc., throughout the Middle Ages, and this despite the fact that, with the exception of the *Asclepius*, the *Corpus Hermeticum* was unknown. At the same time, an inspired imagery unfolded in both Latin and Arabic literature in a succession of "visionary recitals" (as Henry Corbin calls them), constellated around this key figure. The ancient belief that Hermes was the founder of a city was much repeated, notably in the *Picatrix*, an Arabic text probably written in the tenth century, then translated into Latin. We learn there that Hermes was the first to construct statues, with which he was able to control the course of the Nile in relation to the movements of the moon; also a city, whose richly symbolic description has not yet yielded up all its secrets.

This literature, especially the Arabic part, is full of scenarios presenting a personage who discovers in a tomb of Hermes, beneath a stele, revelations of theosophy, astrology, and alchemy. Most of the texts employ the same topos: the First Hermes, who lived before the Deluge, foresaw the coming disaster; before the world was destroyed, he built the pyramids to enshrine the secrets of the sciences. This is the story as told in the *Book of Crates*, an Arabic text dating at the earliest from the sixth century. These texts, often very beautiful, also bear witness to the important role played by Egyptian local color and Greek influence in the Arab imagination after the coming of Islam to Egypt, that is, from 640 onwards. The short but very famous text of the *Emerald Tablet* ascribed to Hermes Trismegistus belongs to this literature; it is part of a group of writings in which Apollonius of Tyana rivals Hermes in importance. These two names are sometimes associated, for instance in the extraordinary *Book of the Secrets of Creation*, written at the latest in 750 and at the earliest in the sixth century.

In the Latin countries, one should mention the romance of Perceval where the hermit named Trevizrent—that is, "threefold knowledge"—reveals the history of the Graal. Modern research has suggested a possible origin of the word "Graal" in the Greek *krater* (bowl), referring to the Bowl of Hermes of which the *Corpus Hermeticum* makes mention. Among the Saracen gods there is, moreover, a "Tervagant" who has been identified as our "Hermes ter maximus," and who appears notably in the *Mystery of Barlaam and Josaphat* (sixth century).

Hermes has a most significant place in the Islamic tradition. Admittedly, his name does not appear in the Quran; but the hagiographers and historians of the first centuries of the Hegira quickly identified him with Idris, the *nabi* mentioned twice in the sacred book (19.57; 21.85). This is the Idris whom God "exalted to a lofty station," and whom the Arabs also recognize as Enoch (cf. Genesis 5.18–24). Idris/Hermes is called "Thrice Wise," because he was threefold. The first of the name, comparable to Thoth, was a "civilizing hero," an initiator into the mysteries of the divine science and wisdom that animate the world: he carved the principles of this sacred science in hieroglyphs. (Even the Arabic term for "pyramid," *haram*, is connected with the name of Hermes, *Hirmis*.) The second Hermes, who lived in Babylon after the Deluge, was the initiator of Pythagoras. The third one was the first teacher of alchemy. Thus the figure of Hermes links Muslim consciousness with the pagan past; but it is no more graspable than that of our Western Trismegistus. "A faceless prophet," writes the Islamicist Pierre Lory, from whom I have borrowed the elements of this synthesis, Hermes possesses no concrete or salient characteristics, differing in this regard from most of the major figures of the Bible and the Quran.

It is no different in the *Corpus Hermeticum*, which presents Hermes sometimes as a god, sometimes as a sage, and at other times as a disciple of the *Nous* or Divine Intellect. According to the Arab tradition, his life is simultaneously physical and transtemporal, after the example of Elijah's, and even in his body he manifests a state of eternity. Pierre Lory recalls that Idris/Hermes is said to have written poems, particularly odes, in Arabic, Hebrew, and Syriac; thus he rises "above sectarian divisions, transcends religious mysteries and chronological time," and speaks "the languages of heaven, of earth, and of man in the integral state, namely Arabic." The *Emerald Tablet* is known to have been transmitted in that language. Lastly, this personage belongs to a delightful tradition, a magnificent example of the myth of the "redeemed Redeemer": A certain angel, having incurred the divine wrath, had had one of his wings cut off and found himself exiled on a desert island. He went to beg Hermes/Idris to intercede with God on his behalf. After Hermes/Idris had succeeded in this mission, the angel gave him the power to enter Heaven while still living in the Seventh Sphere.

It is scarcely surprising that Hermes, whether or not qualified as Trismegistus, was considered as the founder of alchemy as early as Alexandrian times. Greek, which is to say Alexandrian, alchemy certainly disappeared towards the sixth century, but from the seventh and eighth centuries onwards the Arabs took up the thread.

It was their translations of these Greek Hermetic texts that were the main inspiration of the Latin-speaking authors of the twelfth century and after, the period of alchemy's blossoming in Europe. Very many writers on the Great Work, whether Arabic or Latin, even up to the twentieth century, use the name of Hermes or Mercury not only as that of a personage, but, especially in the case of Mercury, to designate a substance or property of things, in expressions like "Mercurial spirit." Mercurius is both the "first matter" and the "last matter," and even the alchemical process itself. As an entity, he is "mediator" and "savior"—C. G. Jung would call him the Mercury of the Unconscious. As the substance of the Arcanum, he is mercury, water, fire, the celestial light of revelation; he is soul, life-principle, air, hermaphrodite, both *puer* and *senex*. He is the *tertium datum*.

The Mercury of alchemical literature belongs to an uninterrupted tradition of attributing metaphysical significances to the gods and goddesses of Parnassus. Thus at the end of the pagan era in the first century CE, the Greek Cornutus, in his *Commentary on the Nature of the Gods*, explains the phallic attributes of Mercurius Quadratus as signifying the plenitude and fertility of reason. The Neoplatonists went further, applying this method to all religious traditions, even foreign ones, and considering the whole universe as a great myth from which our intelligence is responsible for extracting the spiritual meaning. Such was the method, for example, of the Emperor Julian's friend Sallustius, in his book *On the Gods and the World*.

The Metamorphoses of Hermes in the High Middle Ages

The wealth of archetypes which make up the figure of Hermes prevented him from being limited to the Trismegistus type alone. The Parnassian Mercury was well installed in the Christian imagination, not without undergoing some of the curious transformations to which his versatility inclines him. On one hand he was condemned, ridiculed, and turned into a devil; on the other, he was recognized as a benefactor, an exemplar of humane values and Christian virtues, even an image of Christ, while also being the repository of an esoteric philosophy. Leaving aside the last element, we can see certain consistent traits emerging from the Medieval imagery. First there is the allegorical meaning of Mercury as *sermo* (speech) or *ratio* (reason), frequently alluded to by the compilers and lexicographers up to the Renaissance. This allowed Mercury to enter Christendom through the back door, as the god of eloquence. There is nothing surprising in this if one remembers that primitive and even Medieval Christianity was willing to see in Greek mythology a propaedeutic to the true, revealed religion, and to search these tales of Antiquity in the hope of uncovering prophecies pointing to the Gospel. From the very first centuries, Hermes-logos was compared to Christus-logos (e.g., by Justinian, *Apologia* I, 22, and several passages in Clement of Alexandria), possibly influenced by Origen (*Contra Celsum* IV). Hermes was seen as a god of flocks, a Good Shepherd, as one can see from primitive Christian representations where he appears in the form of Hermes Kriophoros, i.e., carrying a ram or ewe. This trait is inseparable from his function of psychopomp or conductor of souls, an obvious attribute of Christ: hence the fairly widespread tendency to represent this mercurial psychopomp as an *angelus bonus*, one of whose avatars, especially in the folklore of Eastern Christendom, is none other than the Archangel Michael—or Gabriel.

Mercury as archangel sometimes appears in the iconography with the head of a dog, thanks to a tradition that goes back to the Egyptian Anubis (cf. Hermanubis!); one finds several echoes of this in the Latin world, notably in Isidore of Seville. Three centuries later, the *De rerum naturis* of Rhabanus Maurus (ninth century) shows a dog-headed Mercury among a dozen other divinities. He holds a rod; a bird seems to be wedged between his legs (the artist's fault, not realizing that there should be talaria or heel-wings); a serpent lies at his feet (a deformation of the caduceus). On the copy of an Arabic work of Kazwînî the talaria are attached to his belt, and the wings on his hat have turned into a cock's crest. On another illustration of the Albrician type, the wings have hypertrophied to the point of covering his legs and head, forming a sort of heraldic cape. Again, in one of the drawings published by Jean Seznec, the caduceus is replaced by a two-light candelabrum.

Such fantastic metamorphoses were due to erroneous readings or interpretations. Perhaps they encouraged the Church to demonize Hermes-Mercury, or rather to diabolize him, in frequent representations as a malefic character. So the reflection of Christus-logos is sometimes a soldier in the legions of Hell! As early as the fourth century, Sulpicius Severus reports that two demons approached Saint Martin: "one was supposedly Jupiter, the other Mercury." The latter was the more dangerous one, for *"Mercurium maxime patiebatur infestum"*—"he was most afflicted by troublesome Mercury." And the author adds that Satan himself likes to take on the form of Mercury (*Dialogus* I–II–II, VI, 4; XIII, 6; IX, 1). The same idea occurs in Martin of Bracarus (sixth century). But was it not Plato himself who set the example? Think of the passages in the *Republic* on the immoralities of the gods. This criticism was taken up by Lactantius and echoed in various ways, for instance in the sixth-century *Barlaam and Josaphat*, already mentioned, where Hermes appears as thief, liar, and libertine; and in the thirteenth-century *Golden Legend* of Jacques de Voragine, which repeats the accusation of Sulpicius Severus.

Yet there is none of this in one of the favorite works of the High Middle Ages, the *De nuptiis Mercurii et Philologiae* (The Marriage of Philology and Mercury) of Martianus Capella (fifth century), which enjoyed a great reputation as late as the seventeenth century. This text—which like most literary works of the Middle Ages up to Rabelais are quoted here from Ludwig Schrader's study—contributed to the fixation, in more or less definitive form, of most of the allegorical features that would henceforth mark the European Mercury. In this tale of his wedding, Mercury stands for eloquence; Philology, for love, wisdom, and reason; the seven Liberal Arts act as bridesmaids. Divorced, the two of them are condemned to sterility: Mercury has no more to say, while Philology has no way to express herself. Presiding over the assembly of the gods at the marriage, Jupiter says of Mercury:

nam nostra ille fides, sermo, benignitas
ac verus genius. fida recursio
interpretesque menae mentis, o noûs socer.

he is our lyre, our speech, our kindness
and true genius, our trusty returning
and interpreter of our mind, O kinsman Nous.

United for a long literary posterity, the couple of Mercury and Philology passed into the poetry of the Goliards, a little known genre but one whose influence was widespread and long-lived. And clearly, it was with the allegories of the *De nuptiis* that the men of the Renaissance liked to play. In the same period, Fulgentius compiled the attributes of Mercury, one of which relates to trade; *"mercium cura"* (taking care of trades!), but he also interpreted the noun as *"medius currens"* (running in the middle).

Unlike his diabolization, but equally unlike the tradition established by Martianus Capella, Mercury even succeeded in becoming a bishop. So one discovers on looking through the illustrations of the treatise on astronomy and astrology of Michael Scot, written in Sicily between 1243 and 1250 under Emperor Frederick II. His attribute here is not a caduceus, but a book. In this context, Fritz Saxl has shown that there was a Babylonian influence, by way of Islam: the pious and learned Mercury of Michael Scot corresponds to Nebo, the writer-god associated with the planet Mercury. Equipped with a book, and sometimes even a halo, the "Mercury" of the Babylonian images was a cleric or dervish, who on coming to the West was naturally made a bishop. In the same way, Jupiter was represented as a judge, on a basis of his ancestry in the god Marduk, who decrees fate.

These accoutrements are due to quite a common Medieval tendency of clothing the gods of paganism in contemporary dress—

and also of imagining the reverse: so that, as Jean Seznec says, the Virgin of Reims looks like a priestess of Vesta! In the choir of the Eremitani of Padua and the capitals of the Doges's Palace in Venice, Mercury takes on the aspect of a professor. And if in Alexander Neckham (died 1217), the planetary gods correspond to the Seven Gifts of the Holy Spirit, and Mercury figures as the dispenser of the *donum pietatis* (gift of piety), this may be one reason among others for his transformation into a bishop. There is a celebrated book, the *Liber imaginum deorum*, possibly by Neckham although it circulated under the name of Albricus, together with a *De deorum imaginibus libellus*, illustrated with pen drawings. Both the *Liber* and the *Libellus* were widely read and frequently copied up to the seventeenth century: they bear witness to a very ancient practice of identifying the gods with the stars, which goes back at least to the Greek poem *Phenomena* of Aratus (fourth century BCE), translated by Cicero (*De natura deorum* II, 15). This poem inspired numerous illustrated manuscripts, known as *Aratea*, from the Carolingian era onwards, which contributed to the identification of gods with stars, hence of Hermes to the planet Mercury. But it was above all the two texts attributed to Albricus, the *Liber* and the *Libellus*, that enabled the Olympians to reconquer their ancient sovereignty.

At the Dawn of the Renaissance

Who was it that guided Dante through Inferno and Purgatory to Paradise? Was not Virgil here a figure of Mercury? Later we will face the problem posed by such equivalences, which is the question of knowing if a name is sufficient to identify a myth. For the present, we will continue to follow the tracks that Hermes-Mercury has marked with his name. Dante himself makes the planets correspond to the Seven Liberal Arts: Dialectic belongs to the sphere of Mercury, Grammar to that of the Moon, etc. But if the fourteenth century opened with the *Divine Comedy*, it also saw the birth of Boccaccio's and Petrarch's works. Italy, moreover, would remain the favorite land of this god until the Renaissance, when he was exalted into a figure of the first magnitude.

Boccaccio sees Hermes as the interpreter of secrets and the dissolver of the clouds of the mind ("*ventos agere Mercurii est*"— "it is Mercury's part to control the winds"). His book *De genealogia deorum*, which would henceforth serve as the obligatory reference work, is perhaps the best example of the borderline between Medieval and Renaissance mythology. Faithful to the spirit of his time, Boccaccio defends the idea that a poem or story always contains hidden meanings, *sub cortice* ("beneath the shell")—a tendency already noticeable in Rhabanus Maurus. He has a particular interest in the identification of each planet with a god or goddess: Boccaccio explains that the planet Mercury is characterized by its flexible nature, exhaustively describing its attributes which are naturally also those of the god. Boccaccio has five Mercurys: the Planet, the Physician, the Orator, the Trader, and the Thief.

Petrarch, on the other hand, initiates a tendency to detach Hermes from an allegorical and interpretative context. But he made great use of Albricus in writing his Latin poem *Africa*. A little earlier there is the *Ovid moralized* (circa 1328 or 1340) of Pierre Bersuire, a work accompanied by several commentaries by different authors. Here Mercury appears as the patron of eloquence and of good preachers, but also of "false indoctrinators."

The works of Dante, Boccaccio, and Petrarch qualify as learned literature. But the popular representations of the gods also enjoyed increasing success in the fourteenth century. Up to the twelfth century, astrological knowledge among Western clerics was virtually limited to Macrobius's *Commentarium in Sommium Scipionis* (Commentary on the Dream of Scipio, circa 400 CE), the writings of Firmicus Maternus, and the Latin commentaries on the *Timaeus*. Then began the translation into Latin of numerous Arabic texts, and almost immediately, astrology began to enjoy unprecedented popularity. These translations, mostly made by Jews, supported an increasing level of interest which can be measured by the proliferation of calendars, almanacs, and *Prognostica*. In this burgeoning of astrological imagery, Mercury naturally held an important place. There are in particular two unprecedented types of image: first, the *melothesia*, which show the astrological signs, mainly those of the zodiac, distributed on the human body; second, planetary images representing the divinities attributed to each of the seven planets, whence the host of images of Mercury. These planetary allegories usually show the divinity in a chariot, above a group of figures known as his or her "children," hence the name "Children of the Planets" that is given to this widespread iconographical genre, of which many complete documents have survived to the present. In these drawings, the "children of Mercury" are persons who supposedly represent the human characteristics of this god; they are shown in series or in groups, presided over by Mercury, who rules them from his chariot at the top of the picture. His children have the attributes of musicians, conjurers, scribes, merchants, etc.: in other words, of all those traditionally placed under mercurial rulership. We find Children of the Planets not only in illustrated manuscripts, but also, in Italy, in sacred and secular monumental groups, especially frescoes.

These children proliferated further in the fifteenth century, when one finds the famous Tarot of Mantegna (circa 1460). A truly initiatic work, this set of *tarocchi* is structured as a ladder of meditations, embodying the spiritual speculations of Johannes Climacus, Dante, and Saint Thomas Aquinas. The Mercury (card no. XXII) is famous, with his triangular hat, buskins (soft boots), flute, and caduceus whose two serpents are replaced by two winged creatures resembling dragons; beneath his feet lies the decapitated head of Argus. This Mercury results from a combination of the Hermes of Antiquity and the Medieval one transmitted by Albricus. But the drawing as a whole was inspired, as Fritz Saxl has shown, by a Greek bas-relief discovered a few years earlier by Cyriacus of Ancona, who had adopted Hermes as his personal divinity. Many copies of this bas-relief had passed from hand to hand, and various adaptations had spread in Italian art, before the *tarocchi* adopted it. The latter served, in turn, to illustrate the manuscript of a poem of

Ludovico Lazarelli, *De gentilium deorum imaginibus* (1471). Jean Seznec has recognized the Mercury of Mantegna's Tarot "in the Cassoni, in the Virgil of the Riccardiana, in a medal of Nicolà Fiorentino for Lorenzo Tornabuoni; in a wood-engraving illustrating the Metamorphoses," and in the interesting Mercury of the Arsenal Library in Paris, where he is flanked by the sleeping Argus and by a bull with its side open like a window, from which Io peers out. Finally, he takes his place with Apollo, Pallas, and Peace among the four beautiful statues by Jacopo Sansovino in Venice, wearing a tunic, a triangular hat, and buskins, and holding his foot on the head of Argus, exactly like the Mercury of the Tarocchi.

None of these motifs is false to the traditional representation, any more than is the Mercury of Mantegna. In the second half of the fifteenth century, the gods were being reintegrated into their primitive form, which, as one can see, was often modified in fantastic fashion. The Renaissance was, after all, more a period of synthesis than of resurrection. An enriching contribution also began to come from the Germanic side. Aby Warburg has shown how the Hermes of Cyriacus of Ancona was adapted by Albrecht Dürer, then by Hans Burgkmair; then popularized, thanks to a calendar of Lübeck, and finally used as a decorative motif on the façades of German and Austrian houses. Thus we can see the North reintegrating the gods in their traditional forms and attributes, at the same time as frescoes such as those of Francesco Cossa in the Schifanoia Palace of Ferrara (circa 1470) continued to extend a friendly welcome to the planetary gods and their "children."

Let us pause awhile to consider the *Primavera* of Botticelli (circa 1480). It evokes the Hermes who is the traditional leader of the Graces, but also recalls Virgil's description of the lively messenger of the gods, who with his magic wand commands the winds and clouds, flying through them like a bird. At the same time, he looks like a pensive divinity, with a touch of melancholy about him (in the Ficinian sense): a god of eloquence, but also a god of silence and meditation. This is why the Humanists saw in him the patron of the penetrating intellect of grammarians and metaphysicians, who, as Marsilio Ficino says, recall the mind to celestial things by the power of reason (*Opera*, p.1559). As Boccaccio wrote "*ventos agere Mercurii est*," so Botticelli paints him dissipating the clouds of the mind and playing with them (cf. *Aeneid* IV, 223) like a Platonic hierophant, stirring the wispy vapors so that the Truth may filter down from heaven, penetrating to us without blinding us. If he is looking pensively towards this heaven, we suspect that it is not with the object of losing himself there forever, but with the Ficinian intention of return, of reentering the world with the impetuosity of Zephyrus (who appears on the right of the painting). For Mercury and Zephyrus, as Edgar Wind recognized, are but the two phases of a single process: that which descends to earth as the breath of passion, returns again to heaven in the spirit of contemplation. The picture thus embodies the three phases of the Hermetic process: *emanatio, conversio, remeatio*; emanation or procession in the descent of Zephyr towards Flora, conversion in the dance of the Graces, and reascension in the figure of Mercury.

Mercury is cited by name in the mystery plays, such as the *Conversion of Saint Denys*, or Greban's *Mystery of the Passion*. He plays a remarkable and dishonorable role in the *Geu des trois Mages*, where his name is given to King Herod's counselor: perhaps a reminiscence of that other function which he exercised with Osiris, according to Saint Augustine, and surely a persistence of the Medieval heritage which had given his name to the devil. In the well-known legend of the Emperor Julian, he unequivocally represents a demon. This tells that Julian's mother-in-law found a statue of Mercury in the Tiber; Julian sold his soul to this entity, and thanks to his diabolical servant became first apostate, then emperor. Incidentally, and in contrast, the second part of the legend brings on a "Saint Mercury" who is none other than the counterpart of Saint Sergius of the Armenian Church, as well as an avatar of Hermes the psychopomp.

Hermes and the New Spirit of Humanism

In the sixteenth century, the image of Hermes made its way through the Italian encyclopedias, which forthwith became classic and obligatory reference books. The essential ones, more or less inspired by Boccaccio's *De genealogia deorum*, are the dictionaries of ancient mythology by the Germans Georg Pictor (*Theologia Mythologica*, 1532), Albricius (*Allegoricae poeticae*, 1520), Natale Conti (*Mythologia sive explicationum fabularum libri decem*, Venice, 1551), Lilio Gyraldi (*De deis gentium varia et multiplex historia*, Basel, 1548), and Vicenzo Cartari (*Le imagini colla posizione degli Dei degli antichi*, Venice, 1556). The almost surrealistic illustrations of Cartari's book revive the fantastic and syncretic vein that had almost been lost in the preceding century: his images of Hermes are both extraordinary and varied. More classical are the emblems of Achilles Bocchi (*Questiones symbolicae*, Bologna, 1555), among which appears a Hermes holding in one hand a seven-branched candelabrum, with his other index finger to his lips in the gesture of Harpocrates: a strange oxymoron, applied to the god of eloquence! In the *Emblematum liber* of Alciati (1531), Hermes personifies wisdom; and Junius, the famous emblematist, studies all his attributes (*Insignia Mercurii quid?*). Fine examples of Mercury are also to be seen in the *Inscriptiones sacrosanctae vetustatis* (1534) of Petrus Apianus. Almost all the mythographers of this time based their work primarily on the last representatives of paganism in Egypt and the Near East, at the same time as archeological documents were coming to light in many places and in unprecedented numbers.

What finds there were! A year after the first Latin translation of the Homeric Hymn to Hermes, Polydore Virgil's *De rerum inventoribus* came off the press, containing a great number of ancient traditions concerning this god. In 1499, it was the turn of the *Marriage of Mercury and Philology* to be published for the first time, and by 1599 there were eight editions of it. There was of course the translation of the *Corpus Hermeticum* by Marsilio Ficino. Hermes-Mercury has probably never been more talked of than in the sixteenth century. Erasmus, in his *Adages*, gives us an inkling of this: commenting on the expression *"Mercurius venit"* (as one now says "an angel passed"), he alludes to the silence of reflection, which contributes to Mercury's identification with the archangel Michael. The *Adages* have inspired quite a few emblems. In his *Praise of Folly* (1509), he calls Mercury the inventor of tricks or of conjuring (*"Quos nos ludos exhibet furtis ac praestigiis Hermes!"*—"What entertainments does Hermes show us, with his tricks and sleight-of-hand?"), rather as Isidore of Seville did long before. But it is as *ratio* and *sermo* ("reason" and "speech") that Mercury enters many of these dictionaries, with the neat formula *quasi medius currens* ("as if running in the middle") serving to explain him etymologically. This is found in Johannes Balbus (*Catholicon*, 1490), Ambrosius Calepinus (*Dictionarium*, 1510), Georg Pistorius (*Theologia mythologica*, 1532), Caelius Rhodoginus (*Lectionum antiquarum libri XII*, 1517), Guillaume Budé, and Gyraldi as cited above. For Budé, Hermes represents the very principle of Humanism, and as mediator he is paralleled with Jesus Christ. In Giovani Pontano's *Charon* (1491) and in his *Urania* (in *Opera*, 1505), Mercury gives his opinions concerning ecclesiastical and theological matters; he evinces a great erudition and speaks about his own reception in the literature of the Renaissance! For Bonaventure des Périers (*Cymbalum Mundi*, 1537), Hermes is now a guide of the dead, now a thief, now an alchemist—or an expert in rhetoric.

In *Baldus* (1517), a Latin epic by Teofilo Folengo (quoted by Ludwig Schrader), Baldus is a Mars-figure who finds himself imprisoned in Mantua for five cantos, then rescued, as in the *Iliad*, by the ruse of the Hermes-figure Cingar. The latter then recites a long anaphoric hymn to Hermes, in which almost all the god's attributes appear:

Te patrone meus, pochinas cerno fiatas.
Mercure, qui doctor primarus in arte robandi es;
Namque times ne dum per coeli rura caminas,

Te rapidis jungate furibundus Apollo cavallis,
Et sburlans faciat tibi forsan rumpere collum.
Tu sopra lunarem arcem tua regna locasti,
Per quae tercentum pegorae faciendo bebeum
Pascuntur, grassique boves, asinique ragiantes,
Atque casalenghi porci, gibbique camelli;
Nam tu per mundum vadis faciendo botinos,
Quos introducis coeli sub tecta secundi.
Alatum portat semper tua testa capellum;
Alatum portat semper tua dextra bachettam;
Ac imbassatas patris Jovis undique portas.
Tu mercantiam faciens vadisque redisque.
Tu ventura canis, tibi multum musica gradat,
Tu pacem, si vis, furibunda in gente reponis,
Tu litem, si vis, compana in gente ministras;
Tam bene dulcisonis tua cantat phistula metris,
Quod male delectans ad somnum provocat artus:
Argo centoculus fuit olim mortuus hac re.
Sic, patrone meus, tibi me recomando ladrettum,
Ne triplicem supra forcam me lazzus acojet.

You, my patron, I feel as gentle breezes,
Mercury, who art the first doctor in the art of stealing
But beware, lest while you are traveling the lanes of heaven,
Apollo should meet you with his raging horses,
And bowling you over, might make you break your neck!
You have set your realm above the lunar citadel,
Through which three hundred baa-ing sheep graze,
Also fat cattle, strong [?] asses,
Home-loving swine, and humped camels.
But you go through the world causing meteors,
Which you bring beneath the roof of the second heaven.
Your head always wears a winged hat;
Your leg always wears a winged projection;
Your right hand always carries the fateful wand;
And everywhere you bear the embassies of your father Jupiter.

You come and go as a trader,
You sing of things to come, and music pleases you greatly.
If you wish, you restore peace to those who rage.
If you wish, you cause strife among people.
Your flute plays so well in fine-sounding rhythms,
That you mischievously bring sleep to their limbs.
Hundred-eyed Argus was once killed in this way.
Thus, my patron, I offer myself to you as a thief,
Lest I should be impaled on a three-pronged fork.

In *Lozana Andaluza* (1528) by the Spaniard Francisco Delicade, Hermes appears to the heroine in a dream, to save her from Pluto and Mars. In the same language, the *Dialogo de Mercurio y Caron* (1529) of Alfonso de Valdès describes him as the clear-sighted god, the critical observer *par excellence*, who is well informed in theology and likes to discuss the events of the year! There is a very different profile in Bonaventure des Périers (*Cymbalum mundi*, 1538): in the first three dialogues, he is the object of a satire, a negative Christ-figure—perhaps due to the influence of Rabelais. Does Hermes not also love his liquor, like Panurge, and likewise claim to possess the Philosophers' Stone? And if two tercets of a sonnet of Du Bellay, dedicated to Ronsard, discreetly betray his presence, it is in the works of the latter that one finds the best and most explicit evocation in the sixteenth century of the god of the caduceus: Ronsard's hymn *De Mercure* (Book II, No. 10), inspired by the Homeric hymn, and dedicated to Claude Binet. In verses of the highest quality it recalls the essentials of the Mercurian legend, after the Greeks, and also the psychological traits and activities of the "children" of this planet, not forgetting alchemy. This great variety of attributes does not lead Ronsard to forget the essence of his character:

C'est toi, Prince, qui rends nos esprits très habiles
A trouver une yssue aux choses difficiles,
Ambassadeur, agent, qui ne crains les dangers,
Soit de terre ou de mer, ou de Rois estrangers.

Toujours en action, sans repos ny sans treves.
Pourveu que ton labeur enterpris tu acheves.

It is you, Prince, who empowers our minds
To find a way out of every difficulty.
Ambassador, agent, fearing neither danger
By land or sea, nor any foreign king;
Always busy, without rest or respite,
Whatever you undertake, you achieve it.

We find him in the form of a messenger in *Maistre Pierre Faifeu* (1532) by Charles Boudigné, which opens with an "Epistle of Master Pierre Faifeu, sent to the Angevin Gentlemen by Mercury, Herald and spokesman of the Gods." Perhaps Boudigné got his inspiration from another French book, the *Illustrations de Gaule* (1512) by Jean Lemaire, whose three parts all open with a prologue placed in the mouth of Hermes. In Jean Lemaire's work he appears as the "erstwhile famous God of eloquence, ingenuity and fine invention, herald and spokesman of the gods," and the role he plays there follows the traditional allegory: "Mercury signifies the word, by means of which every doctrine is addressed and conveyed to our understanding [*entendement*]." This last word should be read to mean "clarity," for Hermes rules "all noble and clear understandings of both sexes, which are the Mercurian bond, and who love good reading." One recalls the pleasure of Rabelais, not long after, at the revival of "good literature." Jean Lemaire reinterprets the traditional Mercurian allegory by giving it a sense that was new in the sixteenth century, taken from Lucian's *Charon*: Hermes opens the eyes of his companion Charon, allowing him a great vista over the theater of the world. Already in Boccaccio, *claritas* figured among his attributes, but also flexibility. Jean Lemaire also echoes Boccaccio when he speaks of the "noble God Mercury whose planet is neutral and indifferent: good to the benevolent, evil to the malevolent, master of the imaginative virtue, fantastic and agitating." Nearly all this recurs in the *Discorso sopra li dei de Gentili*

(1602) by Giacomo Zucchi. In his works (see for example *De umbris idearum*, 1582), Giordano Bruno often identifies himself with Mercury, the messenger sent by the Gods in order to reinstate truth, a truth corrupted by the malevolent actions of the bad Mercurys, i.e. the bad (*"nocentes"*) angels mention in the "lamentation" of *Asclepius*. And we should not forget the Mercury of Louis Dorléans (*Le Mercure de Justice*, 1592): here he is presented— rather unconvincingly—as a god of Justice.

Geoffroy Tory and François Rabelais

Geoffroy Tory, also drawing on Boccaccio for his inspiration, gives ample place to Mercury in a strange work, *Champ Fleury* (1529), devoted to a sort of Kabbalah of the Latin alphabet. After recalling the myth of Io, transformed into a cow by Juno and mistreated by the herdsman Argus, then saved by Mercury who puts Argus to sleep and kills him, Tory proposes the following interpretation:

> Mercury playing on his pipe and cutting off the head of Argus should be interpreted here as the diligent man who seeks out the purest of good literature and true science, and employs himself in teaching it to others, both by speech and writing, and repelling and destroying the inveterate barbarism of the unlearned, as we see done today by three noble persons: Erasmus the Hollander; Jacques, Lord of Estaples in Picardy; and Budé the jewel of noble and studious Pharisees, who work night and day at writing for the benefit of the public and the bestowal of perfect Science.

Here Mercury, the messenger of light (Jupiter) comes to rescue Io (literature) from the prison of Argus (intellectual night), the servant of Juno (riches). It is he who breaks the fences, unblocks the circuits, and restores to circulation the knowledge hoarded by the guardians of the established intellectual order (Argus). In other words, he represents the new spirit of Humanism, as Tory conceived it.

Rabelais knew Hermes well. In his poem dedicated to Jean

Bouchet, he calls him the holy patron of Bouchet, since the latter likes to call himself the "traveler of perilous paths." Rabelais knew that Pan was descended from Hermes and Penelope, and had heard tell of the oracle of Hermes at Pharae. He mentions the Fountain of Mercury in Rome and the mercurial plant described by Pliny. He alludes to the Gallic Mercury, to a statue of the god in solid quicksilver, and several times mentions the relevant planet. Ludwig Schrader has furnished an excellent study of this subject, his interest being particularly in Panurge. Schrader shows how this figure was inspired by Cingar de Folenzo, and by other sources so numerous that one would have to give up hope of finding them all. But the essential thing, at least, is that Panurge can be identified with Hermes. When he is telling of his flight from Turkey, Panurge says: "the sponger fell asleep by divine will, or at least by the will of some good Mercury who put to sleep hundred-eyed Argus." Before questioning Raminagrobis, he offers him a cock; he presents Triboullet with a bag made from a tortoise shell. His relations with dogs recall an aspect of Hermes as shepherd; and Panurge, too, carries a ram, that of Dindenault.

Before his visit to the Sibyll of Panzoust, Epistemon realizes with horror that he has forgotten to equip himself with a golden branch. "I have seen to that," replies Panurge. "Here in my game-bag I have a golden rod, together with a fair and merry *carolus* [gold coin]" He also carries a purse, after the example of Hermes Empolaios. Like Ronsard's character, he is a seller of theriac. He knows how to open any door or chest as easily as Ovid's Mercury (*caelestique res virga patefacit*—"he opens things with his heavenly rod"—*Metamorphoses* II, 819). Panurge also seems as well gifted in languages as his model. Nor does he seek after glory. He has the same gift of prediction as his divine patron, and employs it by *praestigium* in dream or poetry. Panurge's cure of Epistemon is more than a skillful piece of surgery: it is the parody of a conjuration. One can see from this that he has the gift of bringing souls back from Hades to the land of the living (in this case, by means of a pomade of resurrection). But he can also push them thither: in the wand with which he keeps Dindenault and his cronies from rescuing themselves, we recognize the stick with which Hermes urges on the souls of the dead (cf. Lucian, *Cataplus*); and with Carpalim and Eusthenes, he lightly gives the *coup-de-grâce* to the enemies lying on the battle-field.

This does not exhaust the resemblances. Tertullian, Eratosthenes, and others have attributed to Hermes a pronounced taste for clothes which is shared by Panurge, especially in his Parisian pranks. Like the Hermes of the Homeric ode, he is keen on eating and drinking. In his *Cataplus*, Lucian revealed that Hermes does not like to stay in the underground world because there is too little to eat there (cf. also Aristophanes, *Pax* and *Plutus*). Panurge is not only a hearty drinker, but his profligacy extends to sexual matters. As we know from Herodotus and Pausanias, Hermes is represented in ithyphallic form (he is even father to Priapus, according to Hyginus). Panurge has secret affairs (Hermes was born from a secret union of Maia and Zeus); he likes to pursue nymphets (like that other little Hermes, Harpo Marx!), and gives the impression of never being the victim of impotence—a malady which, according to Petronius, is cured by Hermes. Likewise, Hermes is the god of one of Panurge's favorite subjects: cuckoldry (cf. Lucian, *Fugitivi*). Rabelais's hero readily identifies himself with his codpiece, which he calls *trismégiste* ("thrice greatest")—an article which also serves in the cure of Epistemon (Panurge "took the head and held it warmly to his codpiece, so that it would not catch a draft"). But *trismégiste* is also the epithet he gives to his bottle ("You must also have the word of the Thrice-Greatest Bottle"). And Panurge, like the Mercury of Martianus Capella, also has trouble in marrying: here Pantagruel takes the role of Apollo, and Raminagrobis that of Zeus.

Lastly, through his medical knowledge Panurge is not only connected to the tradition of Hermetic magic: he also has something of the humanist Hermes, the savant of his time. This does not prevent him from being at the same time a sort of alchemist, for he claims to possess the Philosophers' Stone: "I have a philosophical

stone which sucks money out of purses as the magnet attracts
iron." And in his speech in praise of debtors, he speaks of the "joy
of the alchemists when, after long labors, great care and expense,
they see the metals transmuted in their furnaces." Transmutation,
the goal of the Art of Hermes, is cheerfully parodied in Book IV:
"Haven't I explained to you enough the transmutation of the
elements and the simple symbol between roast and boil, between
boil and roast?"

The Return of Trismegistus at the Renaissance

The interest in Hermes-Mercury in the sixteenth century went
along with a rediscovery of Hermes Trismegistus, who now enjoyed a considerable vogue in Europe, even exceeding that of the
Middle Ages. Suddenly he came to the front of the philosophical
stage, at a moment when—partly thanks to him—those currents
began to come together that would later be called collectively
"esotericism." Two major events enabled esotericism to take on a
specific form. One of these was the discovery of the Jewish Kabbalah,
especially after the Diaspora of 1492. The other was the rediscovery
of the *Corpus Hermeticum*, brought to Florence in about 1460 by
a monk traveling from Macedonia (it had been unknown in the
Middle Ages, except for the *Asclepius*). After Marsilio Ficino's
Latin translation of the *Corpus* (1471) came innumerable editions
in the course of the sixteenth and seventeenth centuries, as well as
commentaries both erudite and enthusiastic by Lefèvre d'Etaples,
Ludovico Lazarelli, Symphorien Champier, Cornelius Agrippa,
Gabriel du Préau, François Foix de Candale, Hannibal Rossel,
Francesco Patrizi, and more.

At the same time there was a frequent tendency to "apollonize"
Hermes Trismegistus, as if to relegate to the background, even to
obliterate, the magical and theurgical aspect of these Alexandrian
texts. Trismegistus's success in the Renaissance certainly profited
from the craze for Mercury, with the result that in the sixteenth
century, Hermes entered forcibly into the cultural imagination
under both forms, to the point of serving as a sort of catch-all.

Finally, we note one of the most remarkable traits of this presence of Trismegistus—which is to say, of Hermetism,* in the precise sense of the term: editions, studies, and commentaries of the *Corpus Hermeticum*—as his irenical aspect. Wherever Hermes passes, religious tolerance prevails.

Thanks to the rich variety of his attributes, and his intermediate position between religious and literary myth, Trismegistus had all the prerequisites for becoming the axial figure of a philosophical history of the human race. We have seen that ancient authors like Strabo, Marcus Manilius, etc., had already presented him as such. Roger Bacon accorded him an important place in this history, albeit a negative one. More than in the Middle Ages, the need was felt in the Renaissance for conceptualizing the idea of "Tradition" (in the esoteric sense, in which it has been understood since the nineteenth century). At that time it was called the *philosophia perennis* (perennial philosophy), a term defined by Agostino Steuco in 1540, in his book *De perenni Philosophia*. The name of Trismegistus is linked inseparably with this. Pico della Mirandola and Marsilio Ficino prepared the way for Steuco by calling Hermes the "first theologian," and speaking of a *prisca theologia* (earliest theology), which began with Mercury and culminated with Plato. The typical roster, or "philosophical" genealogy, took shape as follows: Enoch, Abraham, Noah, Zoroaster, Moses, Hermes Trismegistus, the Brahmins, the Druids, David, Orpheus, Pythagoras, Plato, the Sibyls.

A curious aspect of this Western "Tradition" is that it continually confuses the mythological with the real. The extreme impor-

---

* The use of "Hermetism" prevails now for designating the Alexandrian Hermetic texts (the Hermetica), as well as the works in their wake until the present time, while "Hermeticism" serves to designate much more generally a variety of esoteric "sciences," like alchemy. "Hermeticist" refers to both notions, particular and general (here, above, it connotes the general one); the context alone indicates which one is meant. In the particular narrow sense, "Hermetist" is sometimes used.

tance given to the idea of *prisca philosophica* sowed a certain danger from the start, making the authority of a text or doctrine depend on the guarantee of its great age. The inevitable consequence followed in 1614, when Isaac Casaubon discovered that the Trismegistic texts dated from no earlier than the second and third centuries of the Common Era.

These writings nonetheless enjoyed a long career up to our own day, if a more discreet one; but there was now a tendency to seek elsewhere than in the Hermetic texts for the mythic reference-point that supposedly guaranteed authenticity. This went to the extreme of completely inventing histories and rituals, which may have been reponsible for the appearance of the Rosicrucians at the beginning of the seventeenth century, and of speculative Freemasonry a century later. As for Paracelsus and his followers, and the great Christian theosophy of Germany which manifested with Jacob Boehme, they owe little to neo-Alexandrian Hermeticism, and give only a modest place to Trismegistus.

In 1488, only ten years after the publication of the *Corpus Hermeticum* in Ficino's Latin translation and a dozen years after Botticelli's *Primavera*, an artist inlaid the pavement of Siena Cathedral with a marvelous panel, still visible: it shows Hermes Trismegistus himself in the form of a tall and venerable bearded man, dressed in a robe and cloak, wearing a brimmed miter, and surrounded by various persons, with the inscription *"Hermes Mercurius Trismegistus Contemporaneus Moysii."* Not long after, Pope Alexander VI, the protector of Pico della Mirandola, commanded Pinturicchio to paint a great fresco in the Borgia Apartments of the Vatican, abounding with Hermetic symbols and zodiacal signs: one can see Hermes Trismegistus, for once young and beardless, in the company of Isis and Moses.

Faces of Hermes in the Seventeenth and Eighteenth Centuries

Iconographical representations of Hermes Trismegistus are, however, more rare in the fifteenth and sixteenth centuries than would be expected—at least, this author is aware of no more than ten (see

Chapter 5). Here we will mention only the existence of a Trismegistus by Manos Finiguerra or, rather, by his disciple Bacchio Baldini (circa 1460) in the *Florentine Picture Chronicle* of the British Museum. Mercury, too, appears in this Florentine series, as well as in countless pictures, drawings, and statuary, wherever artists draw on antiquity for their inspiration and subject matter. We cannot possibly cite all the striking and significant works. In sculpture, they range from the delicate and airy Mercury of Giovanni de Bologna in the Galleria of Florence, to the beautiful version of Adriaen de Vries in the National Gallery of Art, Washington. In painting, there is the Hermes of the Mannerist school: in Hendrik Goltzius, Bartholomäus Spranger, Joachim Wtewael, and Cornelius Van Haarlem, in whose *Jupiter punishing Lara*, 1597, Mercury helps Jupiter to tear out the tongue of Lara. There is Dirck Van Barburen's rubicund Hermes (Rijksmuseum, Amsterdam, circa, 1595) who, helping Vulcan to chain Prometheus, gets himself in between the two characters! Then there is Baldung Grien's helmeted and bearded Mercury, and all the multiple variations on the theme of Mercury killing Argus in order to liberate Io, e.g., that of Johann F.-M. Rottenmayr, circa 1690 (Museum of Art, Chicago)— not to mention his perennial appearance in emblems inspired by mythology.

Mercury belongs not only to painting and emblems, but also to the political and literary imagery that follows the course of historic and regional circumstances. This served especially to remythologize, or to remythify, the role bestowed on the sovereign. Thus in England there is the theme of the magician-king or -queen. From Spenser and Elizabeth I until Pope and Queen Anne, the planetary god Mercury was identified with the monarch, often serving to represent his or her magic power. In Spenser's *Fairie Queene* (1590), Gloriana (that is, Elizabeth) revives in the very bosom of Protestantism the Medieval notion of a World-Emperor who will restore the Golden Age by repairing the ravages caused by Adam's Fall. Queen Elizabeth herself did not hesitate to turn for advice to the magus John Dee (author of *Monas Hieroglyphica*, 1564), just as King Arthur took counsel with Merlin. It is to the credit of Douglas

Brooks-Davies that he has drawn attention recently to the conse-quences of the identification, in England, of monarchy and magic, using precisely the images of Mercury and Trismegistus. This identification justified the pretention of realizing an ideal realm or Empire, differing little from the Arthurian model. Here again, different "traditions" came together in an interesting syncretism. On the one hand, following many of his countrymen, Spenser saw England as a kind of Egypt. On the other, the anti-Roman Hermeti-cism of Giordano Bruno (particularly of his book *Spaccio de la bestia triomfante* [The Expulsion of the Triumphant Beast, 1585]) acted as a ferment in this country, where the tradition of the Druids (supposed to be the descendants of Noah by his son Cham) was still kept alive by those in power, and tied to the notion of the king's sacerdotal and magical role. As we have mentioned, the Druids were often included, at this period, in the tradition of the *prisci theologi*, despite the absence of any writings surviving from them—or perhaps because of that. This is why the English monarch, as a more or less complete incarnation of these disparate elements, tends like Mercury to represent a tension between Heaven and Earth, the scepter being regarded as a caduceus, or vice versa. For this reason, too, the Wisdom of Trismegistus is attributed to him or her. In the seventeenth century, and following the work of Spenser, there are numerous works that carry this imagery, such as Ben Johnson's *Mercury vindicated* (1616), a panegyric of the Mer-curial and magical monarch that was performed at Court; and *Il Penseroso* (1645) of Milton, which transmits the idea of a terrestrial and reformed monarchy, evoked by a poet whose role in this instance is that of the visionary intermediary, like an inspired Merlin beside his King Arthur.

These instances, tied to politics and literature and specific to Britain, tend to fuse one Hermes-type in the other. In the visual arts of this period, Mercury is all too often drowned in academicism, relegated to a mere figure among others in the classical evironment. The further one goes from the Renaissance, the more he appears thus. The earlier epoch was expert in the art of giving the gods their attributes and enlivening them with the breath of exuberant life; later, with the help of the conventional style, one loses the authentic flavor, the specific presence, of the Mercurian myth in art.

True, this persisted in esotericism, whether in the form of alchemy, the Neoplatonism of Cambridge (Henry More, Ralph Cudworth), the cosmosophy of Robert Fludd, or the Egyptian Hermeticism made popular by the learned Jesuit Athanasius Kircher (*Oedipus Aegyptiacus*, 1652). Kircher readily associated Kabbalah with Hermeticism, seeing in Hermes, as Ficino had done, the inventor of the hieroglyphs, or of the truths inscribed on the stone obelisks. But no matter how obsessive was the Egyptomania of the literary, artistic, and philosophic imagination of the seventeenth and eighteenth centuries, Hermes played scarcely no role in it beyond that of an obligatory actor.

This does not, of course, apply to the very specific case of Hermes Trismegistus's appearance in translations and re-editions of the *Corpus Hermeticum*, especially in German-speaking countries. His presence in the latter was persistent from the second half of the seventeenth century onwards, whether one considers Hermetism properly so-called, which is linked in those countries to the late appearance of Humanism, or whether it is a question of alchemy. In a curious work symptomatic of the Hermetic revival in Germany (*Conjectaneorum de germanicae gentis originae*, Tübingen, 1684), W. Chr. Kriegsmann attempts to prove, with weighty philological arguments, that Hermes was the founder of the German peoples, associating the Egyptian Thoth with "Theut" and hence "Teutonic." This was a form of revived euhemerism, in which a mythological character appeared not as one of the benefactors of humanity, but as the patron of a race. Not long after, in 1700, the Jesuit Joachim Bouvet, a sinologue, mathematician and musician, was writing enthusiastically to Leibniz about this presence of Hermes: "The *I Ching*," he says, "is like a symbol invented by some extraordinary genius of Antiquity, such as Mercury Trismegistus, to render visible the most abstract principles of all the sciences." We encounter him again in the *Voyages of Cyrus* (1727) of Michael de Ramsay, where he meets Cyrus, among other digressions serving to show that the mythologies of the Egyptians and the Persians were founded on the same principles: "they were merely different names for expressing the same ideas." Eighteenth-century erudition, even more systematic than that of the Renaissance, contributed to the enthusiasm for Hermes and for Hermetism: examples are the monumental *Bibliotheca Graeca* (1705–1728) of Johann Albrecht Fabricius, and the *Historia Philosophiae* (4 vols., 1743) of Jacob Brucker.

It was, in fact, in seventeenth-century Germany that the greatest number of alchemical works were printed with illustrations and figures. Mercury is the best represented of all the gods in this flourishing iconography of Baroque emblems, where the most frequent and natural figure is specifically that of Hermes, far from any academicism (though not without hidden meanings). Here he is at home: he reigns as the master of reconciling polarities, joining opposites, and guiding our active imagination, in numerous examples from Michael Maier's *Atalanta Fugiens* (1617) to Adolph C. Beute's *Philosophische Schaubühne* (1706). Far into the eighteenth century, the Germans continued to depict him in the illustrations of alchemical books: one sees him decked out in Rococo style and décor, for example in the drawings of the *Deutsches Theatrum Chimicum* (1728) of Friedrich Roth-Scholtz, and the *Neue Alchymistische Bibliothek* (1772) of F. J. W. Schröder: also in Jean-Henri Cohaussen's *Lumen novum phosphorus accensum* (1717), Joh. T. Boethius' *Famae alchemicae* (1717), P.-M. von Respur's *Besondere Versuche vom Mineral-Geist* (1772), etc.

In France, where alchemical iconography was less flourishing, Mercury still formed the object of interpretations directly inspired by the "Art of Hermes." We mention here only the most famous French representative of the alchemical interpretation of the "fables" of Antiquity: the Benedictine Antoine-Joseph Pernéty, whose *Fables égyptiennes et grecques dévoilées* (1758, reissued 1786) enjoys considerable success to this day, to judge from several recent reprints. This learned Benedictine borrowed in part from Michael

Maier's commentaries, but amplified and systematized them, following a tradition as old as Olympiodorus which had never quite disappeared: that of interpreting mythology as a coded language containing all the principles of the Great Work. For Dom Pernéty, Mercury's mother Cybele (or Maia) is the "nurse" mentioned in the *Emerald Tablet*, where the text runs *nutrix ejus terra* ("its nurse is the earth"), Cybele having this meaning in Greek. The messages of the gods which Mercury "carries day and night are his circulation in the vessel during the entire course of the Work." Likewise, "the tuning of instruments which Mercury invented indicates the proportions, weights, and measures" of the materials of the Magistery and the degrees of fire. The psychopompic function attributed to him "signifies nothing other than the dissolution and coagulation, fixation and volatilization of the material of the Work." After the putrefaction, the material of the Philosophers takes on all sorts of colors, which disappear at the moment when it coagulates and fixates: "This is Mercury, who killed Argus with a blow from a *stone*"!

Outside the hothouses of practical alchemy, there appeared in Paris in 1719 the first volume of *L'Antiquité expliquée, et représentée en figures*, by Dom Bernard de Montfaucon, a set of great folio volumes which devote a chapter to each of the divinities, with luxurious illustrations showing objects from Antiquity belonging to museums or private collections. This first volume, which accords ample space to Hermes, was enriched in 1724 by the first part of the Supplement, in which he is found in many other ancient guises. Never before, perhaps, had there been such a collection of depictions of Mercury. To leaf through these pages is to learn of the facility with which he blends with other characters to form a single figure, such as Hermathena (Hermes with the head of Minerva), Hermeros, Hermanubis, Hermapocrates, etc. Montfaucon's compilation serves as a reference work even today; but it seems that no book yet exists that assembles the images of Hermes as seen by modern times.

It was also in France that Court de Gébelin devoted a long chapter of his *Monde Primitif* (1773/84) to Hermes. In a frontispiece, Hermes as geometrician consults an assemblage of mathematical symbols beneath a starry sky, accompanied by Minerva. Court de Gébelin's is one of the most serious and likable studies that came out of the French "quest for mysteries" in the eighteenth century. But in 1774, shortly after the publication of Court's first volume, it is in German that the great Johann Gottfried Herder devoted long passages of his first famous book (*Ueber die älteste Urkunde des Menschengeschlechts*, i.e.: On the Most Ancient Document of Mankind) to Hermes Trismegistus and/or Thot, whom he considered as the symbolic founder and inventor of numbers, letters, etc. In addition to that, in 1801 Herder published a poetically inspired dialogue between "Hermes and Pymander" in his journal *Adrastea*, which owes little to the *Corpus Hermeticum* in terms of content, but much more so in terms of style.

French Illuminism, European Romanticism, and the esotericism of the nineteenth and twentieth centuries correspond to various visitations of Hermes, but more through orientation of thought and a certain sensibility than through specific evocation, or invocation, of him. True, these occurred here and there, with the traditional and explicit attributes of Mercury, or precise allusions to Trismegistus, from the Abbé Terrasson's *Séthos* (1731), through André Chénier, to Ballanche's *Essais de palingénésie sociale* (1827/ 29). It was much more the myth of Orpheus, however, that served for explicit references, and as such haunted the Romantic imagination. As Brian Juden has shown, Orpheus was the god beloved of the Romantics. Later, in the Symbolist era, there was the syncretism of Edouard Schuré, who delivered a vibrant homage to Hermes—a blending of Mercurius and Trismegistus—in *Les Grands Initiés* (The Great Initiates, 1889), almost swamping him in clichés and technicolor prose. Shortly before, Anna Kingsford had published her "Hymn to Hermes"—here, just the God with the Caduceus— a rather good poem in prose, in her book *The Perfect Way* (1881). At the same time, the "Thrice Greatest" made his way into the work of a great poet: *Hermes Trismegistos* (1881), one of H. W. Longfellow's most beautiful poems in verse, is a fine piece of Egyptomania; in that nostalgic evotation he is pictured within a highly Egyptianizing setting. It required Carl Gustav Jung to discover a new fruitful perspective on Hermes, this time more from the anthropological point of view. In his essay "The Spirit Mercurius," Jung summarizes the multiple aspects of the alchemical Mercury as follows:

1) Mercurius consists of all conceivable opposites. He is thus quite obviously a duality, but is named a unity in spite of the fact that his innumerable inner contradictions can dramatically fly apart into an equal number of disparate and apparently independent figures.

2) He is both material and spiritual.

3) He is the process by which the lower and material is transformed into the higher and spiritual, and vice versa.

4) He is the devil, a redeeming psychopomp, an evasive trickster, and God's reflection in physical nature.

5) He is also the reflection of a mystical experience of the artifex that coincides with the *opus alchymicum*.

6) As such, he represents on the one hand the self and on the other hand the individuation process and, because of the limitless number of his names, also the collective unconscious. (Hence the designation of Mercurius as *mare nostrum*.)

Among the Jungians, Rafael Lopez-Pedraza and William G. Doty have produced admirable studies (see Bibliography) among other valuable works of the same type treating the gods and goddesses as existing within ourselves and within human society.

Hermesian Perspectives

The fragmentation of Hermes from the Enlightenment to the so-called Decadence, and the almost obsessional presence of Orpheus throughout the long career of Romanticism—an Orpheus who turns out to resemble Hermes like a brother—brings one up against the invariable problem of any serious reflections on myth. In order to detect the presence of a myth, is it sufficient to follow up the proper name belonging to it? In other words, is a myth identifiable by a particular name? At least twice, in Dante's Virgil and Rabelais' Panurge, we have come across Hermes under a pseudonym. We can recognize him equally well in other literary works, and by no means minor ones, such as Thomas Mann's *Zauberberg* (Magic Mountain, 1924). Gilbert Durand, on the other hand, answered this question in the negative, in a valuable and meticulous work of 1985 (see Bibliography), where he evokes the "permanencies and derivations of the myths of Mercury." Saying that a caduceus alone does not make a Mercury, Durand gives the following elements as the essential signals: (a) the power of the very small (it is true that Mercury is sometimes tiny, as in several of Montfaucon's illustrations and alchemical figures; when his phallus is large, it signifies spiritual fecundity); (b) the function of intermediary; (c) the function of conductor of souls.

In this way, Gilbert Durand was able to define a series of "explosions" of Mercury, i.e., moments at which the myth intensifies. The first ones stretch over long periods: half a millenium, or eight hundred years, in Egypt (Thoth); then Greek Antiquity, and Roman Antiquity. But in Rome, Mercury was not really a Latin god: Caesar regarded him as more a Gaulish or Celtic one, as many Celtic temples and place-names attest. He is basically Semitic: Phoenician, Carthaginian, Hebrew, Arab—in other words, linked to peoples inclined to commerce and mobility.

More illustrative of the process of "explosion" are the next four moments, as given by Gilbert Durand: (A) the "Gothic Renaissance" of the thirteenth and early fourteenth centuries, when alchemy flourished with personages such as Arnold of Villanova and Albertus Magnus. Mercury then appeared as the great agent of transmutation, the "intermediary" of the Work, often associated with the moon (silver being the lunar state, and quicksilver the planetary rapidity of that body). This was the age of Saint Bonaventura and of Joachim of Fiore (the ripening of the Age of the Holy Spirit!); but it would all collapse in the fourteenth century, with economic chaos, the Black Death, and the Great Schism. (B)

The Humanist epoch, in which Mercury as intellectual seems to preside over printing and information. Here he is "mercurial" rather than mercurian. But this world collapsed, at the same time as Hermeticism, in the face of the Enlightenment. (C) The end of the eighteenth and beginning of the nineteenth century, when Mercury is ambiguous, veiling as much as he reveals, as in the craze for hieroglyphs and secret societies. Besides, the whole style of the epoch has Mercury's ambiguity: the language of the Enlightenment serves the Illuminists themselves for speaking of obscure matters, until at the end of the nineteenth century scholars such as Marcellin Berthelot (author of *Les Origines de l'Alchimie*, 1885) turn Hermes-Mercury to Promethean purposes by considering alchemy merely as the ancestor of chemistry! The epoch of positivism and materialistic science obviously stands under the patronage of Prometheus. (D) Reacting against this, the epistemological revolution of our time (especially the second half of the twentieth century) calls on intermediaries, extending the relational concept to every field of science and the mind (relativity, pluralism, polarities, polysemiology, information exchange, etc.), and explores the various possible paths of the inner quest as no era ever before. This kind of revival of Hermes favors a form of "angelism," in the sense that Hermes is called a messenger (*angelos*): a Byzantinism, but a creative one, suited to times when institutions are crumbling, and the Barbarians are at the gate of the West.

The reader will perhaps agree that such a view of history stimulates reflection. There is no doubt that it was Hermes who presided over those periods so perceptively singled out by Gilbert Durand. But at the same time, one feels the ambiguity of the very notion of "myth" as applied to a mythological and literary character, whether it is Prometheus or Hermes, Faust or Don Juan. This tracing of Hermes through history, trying to single out the cultural traits which he anonymously inspired, or the signifiers of certain constants of the imagination, comes down in practice to a summary history of esotericism itself—not that the pertinence of that is in question here. This is esotericism as understood from a perspective broad enough to include the Philosophy of Nature, in the Romantic sense, and the synthesizing eclecticism of Pico or Ficino, as well as traditional theosophy and alchemy. The enterprise is a perfectly legitimate one, in so far as esotericism, thus encompassed, is altogether under the sign of Hermes, and considering that this quicksilver god transcends its boundaries (Durand also speaks of the seafaring and commerce of the sixteenth century). But in the process, one runs the risk of a certain number of images disappearing from the canvas, some of them cherished ones, simply because they do not fit the three signalling traits that Durand proposes. It was not "specific" of Hermes to disguise himself as a bishop; to be the founder of Germany; or to double as god (Mercury) and mortal (the Trismegistus of the euhemerists). The two methods are not exclusive: differing in methodology, they complement and enrich one another. One should, and can, discover the name of Hermes-Mercury through every epoch, while at the same time searching for his active presence in places where his name and explicit attributes are wanting.

Court de Gébelin, on the basis of a Celtic etymology, suggested that one read in "Mercury" the words "sign" (*merc*) and "man" (*cur*). Thus he would be the signbearer, the marker, the lighter of beacons; the one who helps us interpret history and our own lives by giving us symbolic landmarks. His signs are never abstract or rigid; their mediating function reflects the nature of *medicurrius* or *medius currens* (as Saint Augustine and Servius said)—of that which "runs between," or "in the middle." "Ever a transitional figure," writes William G. Doty, "Hermes divinizes transition. He calls eternally into question any simplistic gendering, any reductionist separation between this world and another, any other. Hermetically one opens out endlessly, never losing down nor attaining the point of stasis, but always evincing anticipations of futures all the stories of the past have only begun to intimate." These paths and ways, unknown to vagabonds and ideologues, knit together the opposites in ever novel configurations. And if, on the way, Hermes sometimes steals the substance of what his rod touches, it is only to regenerate it through circulation. Thanks to him, the paradoxical Chariot of the Seventh Arcanum of the Tarot can get under way.

Select Bibliography for Chapter 1

Actes del Colloqui Internacional (1985) sobre els valors heurístics de la Figura mítica d'Hermes. Collected work edited by Alain Verjat, in the series ΜΥΘΟΣ of the Grup de Recerca sobre l'Imaginari i Mitocritica (Barcelona: Universitat de Bercelona, Facultat de Filologia, 1986). Contents: Permanences et dérivations du mythe de Mercure (Gilbert Durand); Hermes: entre la mítica y la mística (Andres Irtiz-Oses); Hermes, Theuth i Palamedes protoi heuretai (Josep Antoni Clua); Hermes i la topografia mítica (a propòit d'un versos d'Horaci i Virgili) (Josep Closa); Une lecture hermétique des *Mémoires d'Hadrien* de Marguerite Yourcemnar (Angeles Caamaño); Lecture hermétique des *Mémoires d'Hadrien* de M. Yourcenar (Rosa Castanyer); Lectures herméneutique de Giono (Alicia Piquer); Hermès va à l'école (Margarida Cambra); Hermes en el laberint d'Ariadna (Isabel Pijoan); Lecture de *Moravagine* de Blaise Cendrars (Marie-France Borot); L'Hermès de Graal (Paul-Georges Sansonetti); Cuando Hermes es otro (Javier del Prado); Hermès et le poète (Alain Verjat); Valeurs inquiétantes de la figure de l'étranger (Ana Gonzalez); Rêverie arc-en-ciel sur une hermétique féministe (Didier Coste); L'Echarpe d'Iris (Simone Vierne); Hermès au cinéma: *Notorius* d'A. Hitchcock mythocritiqué (Joan Lorente); Taula rodona: L'Imaginaire du temps présent (G. Durand, S. Vierne, P.-G. Sansonetti).

Françoise Bonardel, *L'Hermétisme* (Paris: P.U.F., 1985; collection "Que Sais-je?").

Barbara Bowen, "Mercury at the Crossroads in Renaissance Emblems," in *Journal of the Warburg and Courtald Institutes* 48 (1985), pp.222–229.

Douglas Brooks-Davies, *The Mercurian Monarch: Magical Politics from Spenser to Pope* (Manchester: Manchester University Press, 1983).

William G. Doty, *Myths of Masculinity* (New York: Crossroad, 1993).

Gilbert Durand, *Science de l'Homme et Tradition ("Le nouvel Esprit anthropologique")* (Paris: Berg International, 1980; collection "L'Isle Verte"; 1st ed., Paris: Sirac, 1975).

———, *Figures mythiques et Visages de l'Oeuvre* (Paris: Berg International, 1979; collection "L'Isle Verte").

———, "Permanence et dérivations du mythe de Mercure," in *Actes del Colloqui Internacional (1985)*... [see above], pp.5–27.

Antoine Faivre, *Accès de l'ésotérisme occidental* (Paris: Gallimard, 1986; collection "Bibliothèque des Sciences Humaines"). English translation: *Access to Western Esotericism* (Albany: State University of New York Press, 1994).

André-Jean Festugière, *La Révélation d'Hermès Trismégiste* (Paris: Les Belles Lettres, 1981, 4 vols.; 1st ed., 1949–1954).

Brian Juden, *Traditions orphiques et tendances mystiques dans le Romantisme français (1800–1855)* (Paris: Klincksieck, 1971).

Carl Gustav Jung, "The Spirit Mercurius," in *Alchemical Studies* (Princeton: Princeton University Press, 1967). The passage quoted is paragraph 284.

Lawrence Kahn, *Hermès passe, ou les ambiguïtés de la communication* (Paris: Maspero, 1978)

Karl Kerényi, *Hermes Guide of Souls (The Mythologem of the Masculine Source of Life)*, trans. Murray Stein (Zurich: Spring Publications, 1976); 1st ed. *Hermes der Seelenführer*; Albae Vigiliae I (Zurich: Rhein Verlag, 1944).

Rafael Lopez-Pedraza, *Hermes and his Children* (Dallas: Spring Publications, 1977).

Pierre Lory, "Hermès/Idris: Prophète et Sage dans la tradition islamique," in *Présence d'Hermès Trismégiste* [see below], pp.100–109.

Mercure à la Renaissance. Collective work presented by M. M. de La Garanderie. Proceedings of the Conference of Lille, 1984. (Paris: H. Champion, 1988). Contents: Mercure dans la mythographie de la Renaissance (Guy Demerson); Hermès théologien et philosophe (Jean François Maillard); Le nom de Mercure, signe du discours humaniste (Gilbert Durand); Mercure dans la tradition ficinienne (Cesare Vasoli); Diversité des fontions de Mercure: l'example de Pontanus (Ludwig Schrader); L'emblématisation de Mercure à la Renaissance (Martine Vasselin); 'La parole est pennigère': Sur un texte de Geoffroy Tory (Claud-Gilbert Dubois); La mythologie antique dans l'oeuvre de Bonaventure De Périers (Wolfgang Boerner); Mercure alchimiste dans la tradition mytho-hermétique (Jean-Françoise Maillard); Mercure et les astronomes . . . à la Renaissance (Isabelle Pantin); Un Mercure baroque? Le *Mercure de Justice* de Louis Dorléans (Daniel Ménager).

Présence d'Hermès Trismégiste, an anthology edited by Antoine Faivre (Paris: Albin Michel, collection "Cahiers de l'Hermétisme," 1988).

Ludwig Schrader, *Panurge und Hermes. Zum Ursprung eines Charakters bei Rabelais* (Bonn: Romanisches Seminar der Universität Bonn, 1958).

Jean Seznec, *La Survivance des Dieux antiques* (Paris: Flammarion, 1980; collection "Idées et Recherches"); revised and corrected from *The Survival of the Pagan Gods* (London, 1940).

Mirko Sladek, *Fragmente der hermetischen Naturphilosophie in der Naturphilosophie der Neuzeit* (Bern: Peter Lang, Publications universitaires européennes, 1984). French version: *L'Etoile d'Hermès: Fragments de Philosophie Hermétique* (Paris: Albin Michel, series "Bibliothèque de l'Hermétisme," 1993).

Ernst Lee Tuveson, *The Avatars of Thrice-Great Hermes: An Approach to Romanticism* (Lewisburg: Bucknell University Press, 1982).

Edgar Wind, *Pagan Mysteries in the Renaissance* (London, 1958. Revised and corrected edition, London: Peregrine Books, 1967).

Frances A. Yates, *Giordano Bruno and the Hermetic Tradition* (London: Routledge & Kegan Paul, 1964).

CHAPTER TWO

The Children of Hermes and the Science of Man

Hermetica and Modern Hermeticism

The Hermetica contain many elements that have been retained in modern Western Hermeticism: a state of mind, a philosophical attitude, a permanent reference to a mythical scenario of fall and regeneration.

This state of mind is, first, characterized by a taste for eclecticism. The Alexandrian Hermetica of the second and third centuries CE, and those of the preceding period, are the result of diverse contributions, of disparate philosophies blended in a melting pot, the theoretical and doctrinal coherence of which is scarcely perceptible. What is apparent in these texts is rather an avid curiosity, ready to feed upon diverse traditions. Similarly, for sixteenth-century Hermeticists,* the *philosophia perennis* continued to be the postulate it was during the preceding eras. This state of mind is also characterized by a preference for will, on a human as well as divine level. In fact, in the Hermetica, the notion frequently arises that God's activity is his will, and that his essence consists in "willing" all things. God has great need of Man, whose proofs of admiration, adoration, praise, reverence, are the delight of heaven and of celestial beings. Similarly, German theosophy emphasizes the primacy of the will in God, and in this respect the influence of Jacob Boehme in German philosophy up to Hegel, Schopenhauer, and even beyond is well known. In pagan gnosis, the will is a necessary attribute of all who would see the light; the would-be philosopher must *want to know*, and it is his will that he calls upon when he evokes intermediary or heavenly spirits.

The state of mind that is here under discussion is also characterized by an apparent contradiction between two different ways of

*See note, page 39.

approaching gnosis. The Hermetica stress equally the importance of two paths that would appear opposites, one optimistic and the other pessimistic. What is called gnostic optimism considers the universe as divine. Since God reveals himself in all things, Man can become godlike; by contemplating and understanding the universe, he can reach the divine, unite with God by absorbing a representation of the universe within his own *mens*. Gnostic pessimism, on the contrary, rejects the world as evil. Both of these tendencies are represented in modern Hermeticism, the second consisting in strongly emphasizing the consequences of the Fall on the present state of nature. Such an apparent contradiction is rich in dialectical tension, and I would like to emphasize that it is not uncommon to find it in the works of one and the same theosophist, for example Louis-Claude de Saint-Martin. There is nothing astonishing in this, since these attitudes are but complementary ways of seeing the universe, both suggesting that in the final analysis Man possesses divine powers that must be regenerated and utilized. It is thus difficult to determine whether a given theosopher is optimistic or pessimistic. A fundamental pessimism would be that of a theosopher who believes in a power of evil ontologically equal to the power of good, but this is hardly ever the case in modern Hermeticism. In any event, both attitudes should be interpreted as a hermeneutical tension rather than a contradiction within the *Corpus*.

These reflections on optimistic and pessimistic attitudes make it easier to understand the philosophical premises of the Hermetica and of modern Hermeticism. In these traditions there is no absolute dualism. For example, what is called "moist nature" in the *Poimandres*, is not presented as an ontological principle; there is deprivation, but not a complete break. This applies equally well, in modern tradition, to Jacob Boehme and other theosophers. There could not be a real dualism, especially as the world below, so complex, is in homological and analogical touch with the worlds above, which are also extremely complex. In the treatise *Nous to Hermes*, Nous addresses Hermes in order to teach him how to attain Gnostic experience. One gets there, he says, by reflecting the universe in one's own spirit; the adept must learn to seize the divine essence of the material universe and imprint it within his psyche. It is possible to do this because Man possesses a divine intellect. It is thus understandable that there is frequently, though often in a very implicit way, a prolific use of mirror symbolism in Hermetic tradition; this theme was reactualized in the Middle Ages by the famous text of the *Tabula Smaragdina* (or *Emerald Tablet*, printed for the first time in 1541). Boehme, then Baader after Novalis, combine these speculations on the speculum with all kinds of considerations on light, the prism, and colors.

The universe, conceived as a system of analogical and dynamic relationships, like a text to be read, decoded, is obviously one of the biggest common denominators within this vast current of thought. An entire aspect of European literature reflects this, but if European romanticisms have done a great deal to accredit this vision of the world, it must be remembered that this vision is often expressed in the Hermetica, numerous texts of which teach the possibility of a knowledge of God through the contemplation of the world. The germ of Paracelsus's thought is already contained in the *Kyranides*. This tendency affirms: *colit qui novit* ("he who knows, cherishes"), and this is what the Pansophists will say in the seventeenth century. Of course this tendency is linked in the Hermetica to another apparently opposite, but ultimately complementary tendency, that God, unknowable, reveals himself through prayer and religion (*novit qui colit*—"he who loves, knows") In the twilight of the Middle Ages, *Pistis* and *Sophia*—belief and knowledge—try to reconcile themselves, each to the other; Paracelsus tries to reconcile Christian mysticism with Neoplatonic tradition and with a real philosophy of nature, preparing the way for Rosicrucian thought and eighteenth-century Illuminism.

Because the universe is a forest of symbols, it is natural to wish to examine closely all that it contains. Whereas Aristotelianism had a tendency to be interested in the general, the Hermetic showed an extremely pronounced taste for the particular, for the hidden face and form in beings and in objects. Thus the *Kyranides* reflect the Hellenistic and Greco-Roman interest in the *mirabilia*, emphasizing especially the relationships among the seven planets, metals, plants. It is this tradition that has been reactivated by the Paracelsianism so ably studied by Allen G. Debus. Thanks to Paracelsianism, one also sees experimental science making real progress, as abstract theories increasingly make way for concrete experimentation. Influenced by this new Hermesian approach, science is no longer disinterested; it looks for practical applications and ceases to neglect the particular in favor of the general. Another manifestation of this major aspect of modern Western Hermeticism is the romantic *Naturphilosophie*, especially in Germany during the second half of the eighteenth and the first half of the nineteenth centuries. Novalis, G. H. von Schubert, H. Steffens, J. W. Ritter, and many others try, through their research and their writings, to understand and reveal the hidden structure of things by a synthetic approach, but always using nature as a point of departure. It happens, for instance with Schelling, that theory precedes experimentation, but one is not conceivable without the other, which constantly revitalizes an active mind and imagination applied to decoding all the given premises of reality. The discoveries of chemistry, physics, and particularly the new experiments dealing with oxygen, galvanism, and electricity, lead to a form of cosmology or cosmosophy that brings to mind, although in a different style, the world harmonies of Renaissance Hermeticism.

Thus one of the main characteristics common to the Hermetica and to the entire modern Hermesian current is this taste for the concrete, tied to a philosophy of incarnation. The nightmare of Illuminism in the eighteenth century is not the thought of Condorcet or Rousseau, but pure abstraction, the disincarnate systems of certain representatives of the Enlightenment. The Hermetica teach that "there is nothing invisible, even among the incorporeals," because the reproduction of matter is "an eternal operation." The incarnation is "a force in action"; there must necessarily exist bodies that serve as vessels and as instruments of immortal and eternal forces (Tract XI, *Asclepius*; Fragment IV of Stobaeus).

The third major point of agreement between the Hermetica and modern Hermeticism is a permanent reference, implicit or explicit, to the mythic themes of Fall and reintegration. To retell the myth and draw philosophical and practical consequences from it, to reenact it through a narrative or by an inspired commentary, is the task of theosophy. It is interesting to note that the theme of Man's Fall by the inducement of the tangible—a very common theme in Christian theosophy at least since Boehme—exists in the *Poimandres* where one sees that the incarceration of Adam in the tangible was due to eros. It is also interesting to remember that this text is the first among all the Hermetica in their traditional presentation; thus the collection starts with this basic mythic narrative, so that one is plunged, from the start, into theosophy. The Fall calls forth a regenerative work, and the characteristic of all Hermesian gnosis is to put the emphasis on human power and will in the climb or reascension. From the Hermetica to the Hermeticism of the twentieth century, each human being is considered to be a potential magus who, by his intellect, can accomplish marvelous actions. One does not talk so much of Man *below* God, as of Man *and* God. Remember here Pico, the *Monas hieroglyphica* of John Dee, and Christian theurgy; the angels that one can evoke are considered to be Man's ancient servants, as Man before the Fall was directly in the presence of God. The Order of the Elect Cohens, of Martinès de Pasqually, is one of the last examples of this kind of theurgic practice.

Apart from "popular Hermetism," as Festugière used to say, represented by astrology and other occult sciences, there is erudite Hermetism, which is what principally interests us here, and which revolves entirely around the idea that Man can discover the divine, on one hand because of theurgic practices, and on the other hand through establishing a mystical relationship between the universe and humanity. One of the basic concepts of Hermetism (Hermetica as well as modern Hermeticism) is that one can regain his divine essence, lost since the Fall, by renewing his links with the divine *mens.* This aspect was strongly emphasized during the Renaissance. The divine essence enclosed within us is not such as to be freed or regenerated at random, but through very precise means, among which are initiations of different sorts. What is taught during these initiations always leads, even by indirect means, to a belief in an astrological cosmos, even though modern astrology tends more and more to separate itself from initiatic processes and to become exclusively a mere form of divination. There is finally in the Hermetica the idea that, thanks to Man, the earth, too, is capable of improving itself, of rediscovering its glorious state of before the Fall, of becoming truly *active.* An extremely fruitful idea that a text of Saint Paul (Romans 8.19–22) has greatly helped to propagate is that Adam dragged nature down with him in his Fall, and consequently nature is capable of being regenerated with Man's help. Here is a possible basis for an ecology founded on metaphysics.

A few reminders concerning the word "Hermeticism" in modern times are perhaps necessary at this point. Obviously, the word does not always appear where this state of mind, these doctrines, and these practices are apparent. In 1614, Casaubon demonstrated that the Hermetica are not so ancient as had been thought, and consequently, until the beginning of the nineteenth century, the word "Hermeticism" had rather a bad connotation. Gradually, "Hermes" and "Hermeticism" came more and more to refer to alchemy or theosophy—or esotericism in the modern sense of the term. The example of Germany is particularly interesting. In general, the Germans had little part in the golden age of European Hermetism, which lasted from Ficino to Kircher. Agrippa wrote before the Reformation and Kircher composed his main works in Rome. During this period humanism made only slight progress in Germanic lands, hampered by the barrier that Lutheranism had erected against it. Alexandrian Hermetism, by its very nature, and as a legacy of ancient Greek literature and thought, remained a subject of study for the humanists. As a consequence, the authors of almost all the great commentaries on the *Corpus Hermeticum* were

French and Italian.

What is most remarkable is that Germanic Hermeticism (not Hermetism) of the sixteenth and seventeenth centuries was essentially "barbaric," in the sense that it did not owe much to the ancient legacy and developed in a more or less autonomous fashion. Hermes Trismegistus was the object of a particular veneration in Valentin Weigel and Cornelius Agrippa, although they made little use of the Hermetica. Paracelsus, J. Boehme, J. G. Gichtel, and most of the representatives of early *Naturphilosophie*, in other words the whole theosophical current that had chosen Germany as its preserver, owed practically nothing to Hermetism. This remained so, despite similarities of thought, a few publications of extracts from the Hermetica, and occasional references in the works of theosophers and Rosicrucians. One may well wonder if the discovery made by Casaubon did not result—either as a consequence, reaction, or compensation—in the reinforcement of the belief in a hidden Tradition, all the more secret or primordial because one could no longer date it. The Rosicrucian vogue, which appeared at the same time as Casaubon's revelation, can perhaps be partially accounted for by such a reaction, as the historian R. C. Zimmermann has recently suggested.

In the Germanic countries, Hermetism at the end of the seventeenth century and at the beginning of the eighteenth appears to have been a manifestation of humanism as well as of esotericism. Not until the beginning of the Enlightenment did Humanism really appear there. One interesting presentation of Hermes Trismegistus at the time was a book by Christian Kriegsmann, published in 1684 at Tübingen, *Conjectaneorum de Germanicae gentis origine, ac Conditore, Hermete Trismegisto, qui S. Moysi est Chanaan . . . Liber unus*. In it the author endeavored to demonstrate by philological arguments that Hermes was the founder of the Germanic peoples. A large place is also given to Hermes Trismegistus in the works of Johan Heinrich Ursinus (*De Zoroastre Bactriano, Hermete Trismegisto*, 1661) and Olaus Borrichius (*Hermetis Aegyptiorum et chemicorum sapientia*, 1674). In the same period, the title of Ehregott Daniel Colberg's work, *Das Platonisch Hermetische Christentum* (1690–91), was a vague reference to both spiritualists and theosophers, against whom the author took up arms, devoting a few pages to the *Corpus Hermeticum*. A little later, Gottfried Arnold made almost no mention of Hermetism in his voluminous history of sects and heresies, and Johan Heinrich Zedler's dictionary, which appeared around 1730, gave only a vague definition of it. Nevertheless, 1706 saw the first complete German translation of the *Poimandres* in Hamburg, with commentaries, by Aletophilus (W. von Metternich?), under the title *Erkenntnüsz der Natur und des sich darin offenbahrenden Gottes*, while Johann Albrecht Fabricius began to publish his monumental *Bibliotheca Graeca* (1705–28), one of the first great surveys of Hellenism in Germany, in which Hermes is much discussed. And Johann Jacob Brucker devoted an entire volume of his popular *Historia critica philosophiae* (1743) to Hermetism—and Hermeticism (theosophy, Rosicrucianism, etc.). Later on, both in Germany and elsewhere one can see a reason for the development of Hermetism and Hermeticism in the second half of the eighteenth century in the following fact: Popular philosophy had spread the idea of reason and of a divine love everywhere apparent (for example, and the work is significant, by Abbé Antoine Noël La Pluche, *Spectacle de la nature*, 8 vols., 1737–50); however, as of about 1750, the sensualism and materialism that develop more and more make one forget this reason and this divine love, leading by way of reaction or rather as a compensation, to a more marked taste for esotericism.

In the nineteenth century, the word "Hermeticism" reappears, associated with Orphism and Pythagoreanism. This, with preromanticism and romanticism, is the time of its real rebirth. Among the authors less often cited than others, and not to speak of German romanticism, let us mention here *La Thréicie* of Quintus Aucler, which recalls the most beautiful passages of *De Harmonia Mundi* of Giorgi; and in the same vein, in 1806, Pierre Jacques Devismes's *Pasilogie*, where one rediscovers cosmic musical harmonies comparable to those of Giorgi and Fludd.

This is not the place to speak of the different forms of the rebirth of Hermeticism in modern times, especially of the ways in which pagan Hermetic wisdom and cabalistic thought were utilized in the nineteenth and twentieth centuries in order to revitalize the Jewish and Christian religions. I will cite only three major transpositions of this type. First, that of Hasidism by Martin Buber, profoundly marked by the Kabbalah; then, the work of Franz von Baader, who took up and refashioned the thought of Boehme and Saint-Martin in an original and creative way, without betraying any of their fundamental theosophical elements. Finally, the transposition, in the domain of modern psychology, of Western Hermeticism by C. G. Jung, who greatly contributed to the awareness in our times of the eminently formative and therapeutic aspects of these doctrines. From all of this there emerges an impression of something that is multiformed, yet sufficiently united in its substance to allow us to examine the forms that, in the midst of these currents, clothe the activity of the god Hermes, this god of exchanges and relationships, this god generous with universal and specific knowledge.

Hermes's Place Today

What then, in the second half of our century, is Hermes's place, or what are the conditions for his return? The Renaissance has done a great deal, especially by the study of the Hermetica, to keep alive the presence of the god with the caduceus, but what is happening today? The beneficial presence of Hermes seems to be perpetually menaced by three dangers. First in the Hermetic literature itself, by partial or nonexistent erudition. Many works are published, but all too often their content constitutes a betrayal of historical reality when reference is made to the texts of the past. Today, historical forgery flourishes, as well as reprints of poorly researched studies, important books badly reprinted or, even when presented in facsimile, not preceded by any introductory notes for the enlightenment of the reader. Second, there is a manipulation of another sort, coming under what one calls Euhemerism, of those malicious writers who, attempting to "disoccultify the occult," think it fit to reduce mythical premises to "rational" events, such as Erich von Däniken's book *Chariots of the Gods*, which interprets biblical hierophanies as traces of extraterrestrial visits. In an insightful work (*Unfinished Animal*, 1977), Theodore Roszak has given a juicy list of such examples that take us further away from a veritable hermeneutics. In *hermeneutics* there is Hermes, but *hermêneuein*, "to explain," is an *explicatio* quite different from that furnished by the new *Hermocopides* or Mutilators of the Herms (to pick up on the image furnished by the events in Athens in the year 415 BCE). In the sense in which Hermeticism is also alchemy, one speaks of it as of an empirical manner of obtaining energetic results for purely utilitarian ends. Finally the third danger, like the second, consists of a confusion of goals. It is confusion that reigns in many circles, especially in the United States but also elsewhere, between initiatic symbolism as a means of spiritual knowledge, and the simple—and legitimate—need for psychic integration. There is today a real hunger for initiations, for real fairs of the occult. It is often difficult in the jungle of societies and of diverse groupings of new religious movements that multiply everywhere and especially in California, where some even call themselves Gnostics and refer sometimes explicitly to Hermetism, to distinguish between those that emerge from a real religious consciousness and those that translate into a simple need for individual and collective therapy. Mass media produce a profusion of pseudo-initiatic discourse, and since all of this remains in a state of fragmentation, one is dealing most frequently with forms of discourse or of images that are more often fantastical than psychologically and spiritually formative or structuring.

And yet, this "wild" imagining testifies to the need for escaping from an official imaginary,* that is to say, from a schizomorphic regime of images, the inadequacies of which are ever more appar-

---

* In the sense that the term *imaginary* has acquired in the humanities—mostly in France (*l'imaginaire, un imaginaire*)—this noun refers to the images, symbols, and myths that underlie and/or permeate a discourse, a conversation, a literary or artistic work, a current of thought, an artistic or political trend, etc., whether consciously or not. In this sense, the word

ent. New medicines, new therapies, are oriented toward another imaginary that is better able to respond to the complexity of reality. This fusion of therapy and traditional sciences, such as one sees in the best of cases (for example, in the work and teaching of Carl Gustav Jung), is no doubt one of the positive developments of our times. If a practitioner and thinker like Jung can recover the heritage of Hermeticism, in the sense of Hermetism as well as of all alchemy in general, it is because he has seen the necessity for the *anthropos* to live with the myth. The Hermeticists of the Renaissance had understood that the reading of the myth is the key to an understanding of art and poetry as well as of science and technology. They placed it in their field of knowledge. There was, therefore, room among them for Hermes, whereas today it is rather Prometheus who reigns, even without our knowledge or when one does not invoke him by name. The risk that our age must take, if it wishes to see the birth of a hew humanism, consists of relearning the place of myth and mystery in our lives and in our field of knowledge. This task was undertaken by the authors of the Hermetica, who mythologized the cosmos; by those of the Renaissance, an age that corresponded to a powerful remythologization. "Remythologization" does not mean the creation of false myths

---

should not be understood to mean "unreal," nor should it be confused with the term "imagination" which refers to a faculty of the mind. I use the term "imaginary" in the context of esotericism because it comes closest to the notion of a "form of thought," and esotericism is a form of thought rather than a doctrine. As for the term *imagination* in its positive esoteric sense, it refers to the "creative imagination" or *imaginatio activa* (see C. G. Jung), as opposed to the "*maîtresse d'erreur et de fausseté*" mocked by Pascal. In theosophies, that imagination is supposed to enable one to have access to the intermediate realms—a mesocosmos between the divine and Nature—that is, to those of the "subtle bodies," angelic or archetypal entities. Thus understood, it corresponds to what Henry Corbin has called the *mundus imaginalis*—the "imaginal world," or simply the "imaginal." More generally, the creative imagination is the visionary faculty that enables one to grasp the multileveled meanings of reality, i.e. of the Holy Writ and of the Book of Nature.

but the refusal of them; it is not sacrificing to ancient or new idols but refusing to idolize history, that is to say, refusing to succumb to the ideologies and pseudophilosophies of history. If Hermeticism today has a role to play, it is that of demystifying, so as to remythify.

To regain the sense of myth, whether within the framework of a constituted religion or outside it, is also to learn or relearn how to "read." What a beautiful lesson so many of the thinkers of the Renaissance teach us, those who knew how to read the book of the world, of Man and of theophanies! They had understood that language starts with reading and passes through it—the reading of myths, of *anthropos* and of the cosmos. Is not the art of memory, so well studied by Frances A. Yates, first of all a means of reading the world so as to interiorize it and, in some sense, to rewrite it within the self? But if it is true that language starts by reading, it must be recognized that, in our age, one no doubt speaks too much of "writing." Formal linguistics exalts "writing" (*"l'écriture"*) as a primary premise for decoding, whereas Man is above all *homo legens*. Writing, Gilbert Durand once remarked, is only the consequence, the "reduced description" (*"le résidu signalétique"*) of reading. And Hermesian reading is an open, in-depth reading, one that lays bare the metalanguages for us, that is to say, the structures of signs and correspondences that only symbolism and myth make it possible to conserve and transmit. To read, to find the depth of things—by looking in the right place. There is a search for depth in Karl Marx, because of the notion of infrastructure, but one-sidedly applied. And the Freudian distinction between the latent content and an apparent symptom also bears witness to an effort tending toward reductionism. The Hermesian spirit is the one that looks for depth where it is, a living place so poetically indicated in the *Emerald Tablet*, that breviary of profundity. Baudelaire, in his sonnet of *Correspondances*, extolled one aspect of this depth:

> *Comme de longs échos qui de loin se confondent*
> *Dans une ténébreuse et profonde unité*
> *Vaste comme la nuit et comme la clarté*

Les parfums, les couleurs et les sons se répondent

Like long echoes that blend far-off
In a unity tenebrous and profound
Vast as night and vast as clarity
Perfumes, colors, and sounds co-respond.

A Hermesian reading of the world is necessarily a plural reading. The caduceus of Hermes is plural because it is constituted of a bipolarity whose symbolism reflects back to a ternary. Hermes is the antitotalitarian god *par excellence*. The currents of thought that interest us here and that go back to him exalt an ethic of completeness rather than one of perfection; an ethic, a philosophy, of plural totality, which signifies a refusal to objectify the problems of the spirit (for example, of evil) into simplistic or abstract concepts that flatten the soul; which also signifies a recognition of the multilayered and hierarchical character of the elements that constitute the human psyche. What psychoanalysis rediscovered, traditional thinkers had always known and repeated: that we have within us different qualitative levels. It is not only a question of the distinctions among body-soul-spirit, or shadow-persona-anima, but also of what, for example, the psychologist Rafael Lopez Pedraza (*Hermes and His Children*, 1977) says: that there are several gods in sexuality, in our psyche, and not just one, contrary to a narrow perspective. The caduceus of Hermes is also the *tertium datum*, the refusal to stay blocked in the logic of identity and in its corollaries of noncontradiction and exclusion of third parties. Hermes, writes William G. Doty, "leads more to questions than to answers: in no single narrative but in a whole patchwork of ways in which the deity was approached in antiquity in literature and the arts, he is uniquely allied with what is frequently named the postmodern condition." Today, this plurality is made evident by, among other things, the effort of all who contribute to the estab-lishment of a planetary dialogue by deprovincializing ethnology (Mircea Eliade) and by showing what is common and irreducible in the great traditions of the Gnosis and the Sacred (Seyyed Hossein

Nasr, *Knowledge and the Sacred*, 1981). To maintain the dialogue between even the most scientific modern experiment and traditional symbolism is what Fritjof Capra (*The Tao of Physics*, 1975) and others after him have done. There are those who, following Friedrich Schlegel who revealed the Orient to Europe, today study symbols, myth, archetypes, and make of comparative mythology a spiritual exercise that leads to a form of knowledge (Joseph Campbell). Alchemy opens a new epistemology (René Alleau) as well as a reappraisal of modern philosophy (François Bonardel), and C. G. Jung has found a place within the modern psyche for the occult and religious heritage of the world.

Is this a new *ratio*, opposed to the one that has held sway until now in our Promethean and triumphant civilization? Rather, it is a different but nonetheless complementary *ratio*, which integrates without excluding, which dynamizes without reducing. The crisis in our human sciences might well be due to the abandonment in anthropology (in the wider sense of the term) of this *ratio hermetica* (Gilbert Durand) and particularly of the principle of similarity that Hermeticism knew so well how to conserve. German culture was for centuries in our modern culture the best conservator of this principle. This *ratio hermetica* means saying first of all that nature is pluralistic and that these pluralities are concrete things. The Baroque and Romanticism are in Germanic countries the two great creative and truly original moments of which these people were capable, and it is probably no accident that the one and the other correspond to a considerable recrudescence of Hermesian thought and activity. From German culture, inspired by this Hermesian science, comes in particular the idea, set out at the beginning of our century by Spengler, of the pluralism of cultures and civilizations; next to the idea of growth and progress, there appears that of decline, of fall. And when Spengler links the time of each organism to the "qualities of the species to which it belongs," one remembers Paracelsus expounding the theory of the *Kraftzeit* "fixed by God for each species." If, on the other hand, pure, official, exact science, teaches objective disinterest, secular neutrality, the *ratio hermetica* teaches a pragmatic interest, a subjectifying interest. Medicine, astrology, magic must "operate" concretely since the Paracelsian type of "High Science" is the knowledge of concrete facts, of *mirabilia*. There is no question of neglecting the other science, naturally, but of simultaneously using both; of not throwing out, as Kepler said, the baby with the bathwater (that is to say, in his context, not to throw overboard astrological knowledge under the pretext that astronomical knowledge is being verified). The *ratio hermetica* also adds a principle of similitude, or participation in entity forces, to the causal determination of Aristotle. The mediator Hermes-Mercurius plays here an essential role inasmuch as either with him or by him the complete break between the subject and object disappears. Unification is brought about by the mediation of an energy principle that is seen to assure order in the cosmos and unification of the subject. This is to show how much Hermeticism can today facilitate comprehension of a multiple reality which, far from limiting itself to a project of flat rationality, would associate the flesh and the flame, as these beautiful lines of Charles Péguy suggest:

> *et le surnaturel est lui-même charnel*
> *Et l'arbre de la Grâce et l'arbre de la Nature*
> *Se sont étreints tous deux comme deux lourdes lianes*
> *Par-dessus les piliers et les temples profanes.*
> *Ils ont articulé leur double ligature.*

> and the supernatural itself is carnal
> And the tree of Grace and the tree of Nature
> Have intertwined like two heavy lianas
> Above the pillars and temples of the profane.
> They have formed their double ligature.

Is this not at the same time a way of evoking the caduceus? Of recognizing in Mercurius the ideal mediator, capable of unlocking antagonistic dualisms that bear witness to a schizomorphic, and thus diminished, imaginary? Hermes mediates between the body and the spirit, sky and earth, God and the World (this is *anima mundi*), passion and reason, the ego and the id, eros and thanatos, animus and anima, heaviness and grace, spirit and matter. Hermeticists have always looked for the epiphanies of the earth to experience the divine in the world. If they see the body as a magical object, mystically linked to the planets and to the elements of nature, it is because they find sense everywhere in things and transcend the illusion of banality, a supremely poetic task. This path is certainly more poetic than ascetic, but if asceticism is the source of technological progress, it is not necessarily a model to follow to experience totality.

Hermeticists had understood that there is everywhere sense in the concrete. In the twentieth century, Gaston Bachelard, thanks to whom the imaginary established its credentials, has affirmed as a postulate that scientific concepts and explanations derive from the pragmatic and not the other way around. In fact, the fear of or the refusal of sense corresponds today to a convulsive jump by Prometheus, who wants to work for Man's benefit by using a usurped light, a torch that is not nature's. But this refusal leads to the agnosticism of the great abstractions, since saying that sense can only be found in formal relations, in abstract form, in the exchange of empty signs, is to recoil from it. Oriented almost entirely toward formalism, linguistics today leads to a consideration of language as being shut off from the outside, without links outside itself, without heuristics. Solipsism, atomization, incommunicability are the ransom of our *episteme* since the eighteenth century, whereas Hermes shows the path of otherness, of living diversity, of communication of souls. This otherness, as well as its opposite—shutting out of the outside—are found in our arts and our literature, according to whether Narcissus or Prometheus reigns as absolute master, or whether, on the contrary, Hermes favors and stimulates living relationships within art and literature. Prometheus without Hermes is dangerous, but so are Narcissus and Dionysus. A god, like a child, should not be left alone when he or she plays. The warning thrown out by Nietzsche in *The Birth of Tragedy*

(1872)—namely that a civilization should not cultivate one god-figure only, but at least two (like Apollo and Dionysus in pre-Socratic Greece)—has shown itself to be even more incontrovertibly true than one had thought. This is so because monotheism without counterpart runs the risk of being transformed into a dangerous philosophical abstraction devoid of links with reality—the words "monotheism" and "polytheism" being used here of course without a theological sense; for example, the Christian belief in angels is a form of polytheism. Pagan gods and Judeo-Christian myths can go well together in a healthy soul, in the same way that they got along well together during the Renaissance, that period of abounding health and supreme vitality.

Magia, understood as a search for the unity of Man with nature, teaches us an active manner of being and having, rather than a method of manipulation. What one calls tradition is not a sort of immutable depository, an invariable doctrinal body, but a perpetual rebirth. The tragedy of a culture occurs when everything is perceived in the form of an empty and abstract concept. This could well be our tragedy.

Select Bibliography for Chapter 2

Françoise Bonardel, L'Hermétisme (Paris: Presses Universitaires de France, 1985).

————, Philosophie de l'Alchimie (Paris: Presses Universitaires de France, 1993).

William G. Doty, Myths of Masculinity (New York: Crossroad, 1993).

Gilbert Durand, Science de l'homme et tradition (Paris: Berg International, 1975).

————, Figures mythiques et visages de l'oeuvre (Paris: Berg International, 1979).

Antoine Faivre, L'Esotérisme au XVIIIème siècle en France et en Allemagne (Paris: Seghers-Laffont, 1974).

————, Accès de l'ésotérisme occidental (Paris: Gallimard, 1986).

Arthur Darby Nock and André-Jean Festugière, ed. and trans., Corpus Hermeticum, 4 vols. (Paris: Les Belles Lettres, 1954–1960).

André-Jean Festugière, La révélation d'Hermès Trismégiste, 3 vols. (Paris: Les Belles Lettres, 1981; 1st ed., 1949–1954).

Carl Gustav Jung, "The Spirit Mercurius" (see detailed reference in bibliography of Chapter 1).

David Miller, The New Polytheism (Dallas: Spring Publications, 1974).

Seyyed Hossein Nasr, Knowledge and the Sacred (Albany: State University of New York, 1981).

Theodore Roszak, Unfinished Animal: The Aquarian Frontier and the Evolution of Consciousness (New York: Harper and Row, 1975).

Mirko Sladek, Fragmente der hermetischen Philosophie in der Neuzeit (Bern: Peter Lang, 1984).

Ernest Lee Tuveson, The Avatars of Thrice-Great Hermes: An Approach to Romanticism (Lewisburg: Bucknell University Press, 1982).

Frances A. Yates, *Giordano Bruno and the Hermetic Tradition* (London: Routledge & Kegan Paul, 1964).

————, *The Art of Memory* (London: Routledge & Kegan Paul, 1966).

Rolf Christian Zimmermann, *Das Weltbild des jungen Goethe*, 2 vols. (Munich: Wilhelm Fink, 1969–1979).

CHAPTER THREE

From Hermes-Mercury to Hermes Trismegistus: The Confluence of Myth and the Mythical

Introduction

The title of this study calls, at the outset, for a precise definition of what is meant by myth, the mythical, and confluence. I use "myth" in the sense understood by anthropology, by comparative religion, and by formalistic and figurative structuralism. A myth is a metahistorical and foundational story concerning the origin, nature, and end of things; or, as is the case here, it is a story, generally initiatic, which features one or more divine heroes. The "mythical" here is everything that is left when explicit reference to the gods is omitted. Examples are literary myths such as those of Don Juan, Faust, Tristan and Isolde, who are not divine personages but belong to our own world;[1] or the mythical in cities or in society, as treated by such as Pierre Sansot or Michel Maffesoli. "Confluence" designates the place of transition between myth and the mythical. Myth necessarily makes use of our own space and time, which favors the transition into the latter, hence into history, of the gods of mythology. Thus Hermes came to leave Olympus and descend from the *illo tempore* of myth to occupy an intermediate space and time under the name of Hermes Trismegistus, and sometimes even to come right down to earth where, as Hermes the god of crossroads, he at least seems less out of place than his peers.

We are not concerned here with the presence of Hermes within ourselves, on the psychological plane, though others have spoken of him in this fashion, such as Ginette Paris, Jean Bolen, William G. Doty, and James Hillman. Mine is the more limited goal of gathering from the documents certain moments at which Hermes has been seen to leave Olympus and pass into the mythical realm, as defined above. Certainly the myth, as Gilbert Durand has recalled it, does not always carry Hermes's proper name; but this will enable us to pinpoint the confluence, the place where two Mercuries become distinguishable and rejoin, or separate and fuse together: they are respectively the Mercury of mythology, and an Egyptian priest of some historical substance: on the one hand, the god of the caduceus;[2] on the other, Hermes Trismegistus, the legendary author of the writings called the Hermetica.

I. Thoth, Hermes, Trismegistus;
or the Ancient Faces of Mercury

A. The Appearance of Trismegistus

The Greeks are known to have given the name of Hermes to Thoth, a local divinity of Middle Egypt, worshipped at Khmonou (now called Achmounein), which they renamed Hermopolis. The assimilation of Thoth to Hermes had become official by the third century BCE, as attested by a decree of the priests of Rosetta (196 BCE): a Hermes in whom Thoth is to be understood under the name of Hermes the Great, the god who helped Horus to reconquer the Delta. From this point onwards, it seems justifiable to see resemblances between Thoth-Hermes and Hermes-Trismegistus. There is nothing fortuitous about their sharing a name in common: Thoth was the magician-god who appeared to Isis while she was trying to bring the members of Osiris back to life; he was also the "hypomnematographer" or secretary of the gods. Even today, Trismegistus has kept this dual function of assembler and maintainer, in an eclecticism inseparable from the Western notion of esotericism, and as the guarantee of a tradition.

There is another striking connection. A little after the decree of 196 BCE, the Jewish writer Artapan assimilated Thoth-Hermes to Moses. The historian of Alexandrian Hermetism, A.-J. Festugière, noticed this same amalgam reappearing in the eighth century CE with Cosmas of Jerusalem, and I will be citing some other comparable instances. This process of transition, by which a god slips into a historical personality, also occurs in the reverse direction: it seems in part to be the result of the activities credited to Thoth-Hermes. Hecateus of Abdera, who calls him Osiris's secretary, attributes to Hermes the invention of writing, astronomy, music, the games of the palaestra, eurhythmy, the three-stringed lyre, the cultivation of the olive—and interpretation. Not long after, taking his inspiration from Hecateus, Artapan tells us more: besides writing, Thoth-Hermes "taught the Egyptians navigation, the lifting of stones with cranes, weapons, water pumps, war machines, and philosophy"![3] In this way, the attributes gradually come together to make up a mythical figure: Hermes Trismegistus. Although it seems that one cannot say exactly when this figure became distinct from Hermes-Mercury, Artapan (circa 200 BCE) is an important reference point.

In addition to this, there was in Egypt from perhaps the third century BCE an esoteric literature in Greek, particularly astrological, part of which seems definitely to have been ascribed to Hermes. This must imply the god Hermes, whose patronage may have increased the prestige of such texts. The Egyptian name of Thoth was such as to confer on them a more mysterious or occult flavor than that of Hermes-Mercury, already so evocative. Thus books of philosophy or theosophy under the name of Hermes could have been in circulation from the first century CE and perhaps even before, though it seems to have been from the third century onwards that they received serious attention.[4] The point in common of all these Hermetic writings or Hermetica, treating astrology, alchemy, and theosophy, is that they present themselves as scriptures revealed by Hermes, who under the name of Hermes Trismegistus puts his definitive stamp—though not without ambiguity—on the so-called "philosophical" Hermetica written in the Delta in the second and third centuries CE. Essentially this means the collection known as the *Corpus Hermeticum*, plus the *Asclepius* and the Fragments known as Stobaeus's.[5] The eighteen treatises of the *Corpus* are variously addressed: some by Hermes to his son and disciple Tat; others by Hermes to his disciple Asclepius and to other disciples; yet others, including the *Poimandres*, by the god Nous (Supreme Intellect) to a personage who may be Hermes, though this name does not appear here, nor in some other treatises.[6] In these theosophic Hermetica, Hermes plays the role of initiator, being the epitome of a master of wisdom. The authors have introduced him not only to adorn their gnosis with the patina of antiquity, but also out of a need to link their doctrine to a sacred tradition.

The author of the twenty-third Fragment of Stobaeus (*The Sacred Book of Hermes Trismegistus*, called *"Pupil of the World"* or *Kore Kosmou*, sometimes published under the title *The Virgin of the World*) describes the court of the Lord, maker of the universe, before mortals lived on the earth. Hermes appears there as "the soul [*psyche*] who possessed the sympathetic link with the mysteries of heaven: that is what Hermes was, who knew all things" (an interesting passage, recalling the biblical Book of Wisdom 7.17ff. and 9.11). God calls Hermes "soul of my soul, sacred intellect of my intellect." But the text does not explain the precise status of this "soul" or this "intellect" which constitute Hermes.[7] It seems to be a case of one of those *psychai* that are not discarnate souls, but a sort of composite organism: probably a subtle body, since Hermes, Isis, and Horus accomplish acts that require a body. In any case, Hermes enjoys a privileged place among these entities, for it is he whom God sends to this lower world to teach it, to make known the *gnôsis* and to abolish *agnôsia* (i.e., voluntary ignorance, whereas *agnôia* is accidental ignorance), by addressing certain select disciples who, like him, are of divine origin—seeing that the earth was so far inhabited only by divine beings: Tat, Asclepius, Imouthes, and Hermes himself. These disciples, destined to perpetuate the Hermetic gnosis in obedience to the divine will, are not really celestial gods, but also not ordinary men, since humanity only appears later. It is more a matter of celestial emanations on the earth, charged with a divine mission, who will return to heaven when their task is done, as is generally told of Isis and Osiris.

The beautiful text of the *Kore Kosmou* adds to this mission of Hermes another one: the Lord, having asked him to assemble the other gods in order to discuss the plan for creating mankind, then asks him to take part in this creation:

> As for me, said Hermes, I declare that I will not only create the nature of mankind, but I will make them the gifts of Wisdom, Temperance, Persuasion, and Truth, and will give myself ceaselessly to Invention; moreover, I will always assist the mortal life of men born under my signs (for the signs attributed to me by the Father and Creator are at least sensible and intelligent), and all the more so, when the movement of the planets that rule them shall be in accord with each one's natural energy.

In this context, it is the planet Mercury who speaks, and as such it is not different from the other six planets. Nevertheless, it is tempting to interpret this text in the sense that Hermes found himself designated by the Master of the universe as his steward and administrator, even to the point of being the principal actor, after the supreme God, on the anthropogonic stage (as also in the text of the *Strasburg Cosmogony*), while Adrastea, the goddess with piercing eyes, is appointed "watcher" of the universe. Hermes is therefore a god, or a soul, or a *psyche*, that has come down as the first divine emanation, while Isis and Osiris represent the second emanation, also sent into this world to teach mankind. But Isis and Osiris were able to teach only because they had rediscovered the writings to which Hermes had consigned his gnosis.

Since Hermes has a progeny, it is difficult to tell in each text which Hermes is intended, and which of them can be identified as Trismegistus. At every epoch, the documents seem to contradict each other. But if the number of Hermeses is variable, and if their identity is unstable, their number is three by definition whenever it is a question of the Trismegistus(es). This inclines to connect the latter with the tricephalus or three-headed Mercury (*tricephalos*, *triplex*), thus named to suggest his belonging to the three worlds: celestial, terrestrial, and infernal or subterranean. The epithet also evokes the three-sided stones erected on roads where three routes meet, which is natural enough, considering that Mercury is a god of the crossroads. Mercury has moreover been depicted with a three-pointed golden wand. Trismegistus, for his part, is "thrice great," *trismegistos* resulting from the marriage of a superlative in the repetitive Egyptian style, as in "great, great" (*megas, megas*). At the end of the third century CE, this superlative was translated into Greek, with reference precisely to Hermes, by the superlative pronounced three times.

However, the coupling of "Hermes" with "Trismegistus" is rarely met with outside the Hermetic texts, that is, scarcely before the second century CE. One cannot fail to associate this epithet with the alchemical ternary. In fact, an Alexandrian alchemist who saw Hermes as the first master of the Work, read his name as indicating that the operation should be done according to a three-fold ontological activity.[7] The *Suda* (=Suidas) recognized it as the sign of the Trinity, an idea supposedly brought to mankind by Hermes. Bernard of Trevisan (*Liber de secretissimo philosophorum opere chemico*, fifteenth century) detects in it an allusion to the three realms, mineral, vegetable, and animal. In a treatise dated 1736 and published under the pseudonym of Pyrophilus, one reads that this number is an allusion to the three alchemical principles of salt, sulphur, and mercury. It is most often interpreted as meaning "great philosopher, priest, and king."[8] We must not forget another Hermes, or rather a homonym of our own: Hermogenes, who is treated in the *Golden Legend* and represented in certain stained-glass windows: he, too, is sometimes "triplex."[9] His name should probably be connected with that of the priest Hermon, spoken of by Galen (IV, 1) in the first century CE, in connection with the making of remedies.

B. Genealogies of the Triplex

I spoke above of slippages and transitions, taking place in more than one direction. Trismegistus is a fictional personage who nonetheless "authored" some important books; his status is ambiguous precisely because he stands at the confluence of myth and the mythical. He is both the precipitation of Mercury into history, and the return of the historical to Olympus. These fluctuations, or if one prefers, this double movement, favors an open genealogy and the presence of more than one Hermes.

The most "classic" genealogy of Hermes in the Hellenistic era was set down in the third or second century BCE. It begins the series of Hermeses with Thoth, who engraved his knowledge on stelae, then hid them. His son was Agathodemon, sometimes credited with the editing of his father's teachings, and their conservation. The son of Agathodemon was the second Hermes, who later, in the second century CE, was often called Trismegistus—although this word is not always enough for his certain identification in the succession of Hermeses. Lastly, the son of Trismegistus was Tat. Nothing is more uncertain than divine genealogies: one even finds Isis as a daughter of Hermes, according to traditions handed down by Plutarch.[10] And however "classic" the above succession may be, it can only serve in certain cases. Cicero, in *De natura deorum* (III, 22), enumerates no fewer than five Mercurys: the son of Heaven and Light; the son of Valens and the nymph Phoronis; the son of Jupiter and Maia; the son of Nilus. The fifth, called "Theyt," is the one whom Cicero seems to intend as Trismegistus, for he says of him: "He is the one worshipped by the Pheneatae (in Arcadia) and who is said to have slain Argus, for which he fled to Egypt and there taught the Egyptians laws and writing." Lactantius later speaks of the son of Jupiter and Maia, but also of the son of Bacchus and Proserpine, and the son of Jupiter and Cyllene!

Relying on different sources still, Saint Augustine in the *City of God* makes Mercury the great-grandson of a contemporary of Moses:

> In [King Saphrus's] time Prometheus (as some hold) lived, who was said to make men out of earth, because he taught them wisdom so excellently well, yet there are no wise men recorded to live in his time. His brother Atlas indeed is said to have been a

great astronomer, whence the fable arose of his supporting heaven upon his shoulders: yet there is an huge mountain of that name, whose height may seem to an ignorant eye to hold up the heavens. And now began Greece to fill the stories with fables . . . Some of the dead kings were recorded for gods, by the vanity and customary superstition of the Greeks . . . and in these times also lived Mercury, Atlas's grandchild, born of Maia his daughter: the story is common. He was a perfect artist in many good inventions, and therefore was believed (at least men desired he should be believed) to be a deity. Hercules lived after this, yet was he about those times of the Argives: some think he lived before Mercury, but I think they are deceived. But, howsoever, the gravest historians that have written of them avouch them both to be men, and that for the good that they did mankind in matter of civility and other necessaries to human estate, were rewarded with those divine honors. (*Civ. Dei.* XVIII, 8)

In the same *City of God*, Augustine suggests an etymology for the name "Mercurius" which he says means *medius currens* (running in the middle), "because language 'runs' like a sort of mediator between men." Elsewhere he returns to the genealogy of Hermes with a reprise of the above, which interests us for two reasons. First, Augustine is a euhemerist in that he sees outstanding human acts (on whose historical reality he casts no doubt) as the origin of the Greek gods; thus Mercury now ascends from humanity to Olympus, whereas before we saw him descend thence to incarnate into a mythical personage. Augustine leaves open the question of whether Hermes Mercury and Hermes Trismegistus were originally one and the same personage, but one has the impression that he thinks so, and that he thinks it a human being. He cites the discourse of Hermes to Asclepius (a text contained in the *Asclepius*), where the latter is presented as the grandson of another Asclepius or Aesculapius. The grandfather is buried in a temple "on a mountain of Libya, not far from the bank of the crocodiles," but from heaven "he now assures the sick of receiving through his superhuman power all the succour which he was wont to give them through his medical art." It is on this occasion that Hermes actually introduces himself to Asclepius as the descendant of another Hermes: "Hermes, my ancestor, whose name I bear . . . " (compare the quotation above). Saint Augustine comments:

> This was Hermes, the elder Mercury, buried (they say) in Hermopolis, the town of his surname. Behold now, here are two new gods already, Aesculapius and Mercury; for the first, the opinion of both Greeks and Latins confirms it. But the second many think was never mortal: yet he says here that he was his grandfather, for this is one and that another, they both have one name. But this I stand not upon: he and Aesculapius were both made gods from men, by this great testimony of his grandson Trismegistus.[11]

In other words, Trismegistus is the grandson of the divine or human Hermes of Hermopolis. One can see how the shift took place: it is this very ancestor whom many other authorities attest to having been Trismegistus, and not the descendant who talks with Asclepius.

The other reason for our interest in the genealogy of Hermes as presented by Augustine is that it would serve more or less as a prototype in the following centuries, copied in this form or presented in a more or less fragmented or contradictory fashion. The book believed to be the earliest Latin work on alchemy, dated 1144, includes a preface by the translator from the Arabic original (Robert of Chester), who writes:

> We read in the ancient histories of the gods that there were three Philosophers who were all called Hermes. The first was Enoch, whose names were also Hermes and Mercury. The second was Noah, also called Hermes and Mercury. The third was the Hermes who ruled Egypt after the Deluge and long occupied that throne. Our predecessors called him Triplex by reason of his threefold

virtue, bestowed on him by God. He was king, philosopher, and prophet. It was this Hermes who after the Deluge was the founder of all the arts and disciplines, both liberal and mechanical.[12]

From the thirteenth century, we call on three witnesses. The *Summa philosophia*, sometimes attributed to Robert Grosseteste, tells us that Atlas had a nephew called Mercury, whose grandson was our hero. The author repeats Saint Augustine's statement, adding to it from other sources.[13] Daniel of Morley distinguishes between "two most excellent authorities," the "great Mercury" and his nephew "Trismegistus Mercurius."[14] Lastly, a Hermetic text that roughly repeats this information adds that the third Hermes was the first to provide an explanation of astronomy.[15]

Naturally all this recurs at the Renaissance. Marsilio Ficino is followed by many other authors, including Ludovico Lazarelli. The latter tells us that Moses was born in *anno mundi* 2374 (1598 BCE):

[At that time] there flourished a most expert Astrologer named Athlas, the brother of Prometheus, a man much esteemed in Physics, and ancestor on the maternal side of the great Mercury, whose nephew was Mercury Trismegistus the present ambassador, surely a man of singular and memorable virtue, a most noble and excellent Mathematician, as Saint Augustine has fully told. [. . . He drew up the characters of laws and letters,] showing them by the figures of beasts and trees, in order to make them easier and more open to understanding. And he was in such high esteem of men for his integrity, goodness, prudence, diligence, knowledge, kindness, and every other virtue in which he was perfect and accomplished, that they spoke of him and placed him among the number of their gods, and built many temples in his name. No one was permitted to use his name, nor to utter it in vulgar speech or in anger, such was the honor and reverence in which he was held. The Egyptians called the first month of the year by his name. They also dedicated to him all the books which they wrote, calling him the inventor of all things, prince, and author of wisdom and eloquence. Likewise he built a city, which to this day bears his own name and is called Hermopolis.[16]

In his handsome book *Symbola aureae mensae duodecim nationum*, published 1617 in Frankfurt, Michael Maier presents twelve characters who defend alchemy against an opponent set on sapping its foundations and its spiritual reality.[17] Presiding over this fictitious "turba" of twelve is Trismegistus, in the place of honor and occupying the entire first chapter of the book. Maier spins the following yarn about him:

Palaephastus, in his Second Book, writes that the father of Hermes or Mercury was Philon. He begat this son of his daughter Proserpine, after beholding her in her bath. Wishing to expose the child [on water, like Moses], because of shame at the incest, he consulted a mathematician celebrated at that time for his predictions and prophecies, who replied to Philon that the son born of his daughter would become a very great and very learned interpreter of divine matters, and that he would win high authority and power among men. This, he said, was a most certain event, promised by the stars. The father, his mind changed by the reply of this sage, preserved his son and had him educated in literature and the liberal arts to the point at which, with time, he was considered by all as a prodigy for his teaching and the acuteness of his intelligence. But no one sees that this story is a fable falsely attributed to Hermes, like that of Mahomet. And there is no need to seek another father for him, seeing that he himself, as has been said, acknowledged Hermes, not Philon, for his father.[18]

Even as late as the eighteenth century, the alchemist F. J. W. Schröder identified Trismegistus with Joseph, while Lenglet de Fresnoy and Michael de Ramsay thought that he was the same as King Siphoas who reigned around 1900 BCE.[19] Dom Pernéty seemed less keen on dispelling an ambiguity favorable to his project of alchemical hermeneutics. If the text of the *Emerald Tablet*, he says, contains the words "*nutrix eius est terra*," it is in allusion to Maia, the mother of Mercury, who is identical to Cybele or the Earth. And the Mercury who conducts the dead to Pluto's realm and draws them back from thence corresponds to the dissolution and coagulation, fixation and volatilization, of the matter of the Work. Pernéty adds a little further on, concerning the five Mercuries of Cicero: "There has never been more than a single Mercury to whom one can credibly attribute all that the fables tell of him; and this Mercury can be none other than that of the Hermetic philosophers."[20]

C. Books and Seals of Hermes

There is no lack of books attributed to Hermes. At about the time when the *Corpus Hermeticum* was being compiled, Manetho reported 36,525 books, and Seleucus, 20,000! Iamblichus, towards 300 CE, suggested a more modest number. The testimony of Clement of Alexandria is instructive, as, writing in the same period as Manetho, he describes a contemporary Egyptian religious service. First appeared the cantor, who had to be able to recite by heart two of the books of Hermes, one containing hymns to the gods. He was followed by a celebrant who carried a palm branch and an instrument for measuring time, who must always have in his memory the *Astrologumena* of the four books of Hermes that treat of the planets. Clement enumerates "forty-two indispensable books of Hermes," of which thirty-six had to be known by heart by certain officiants "because they contain all the wisdom of the Egyptians," while the *pastophoroi* (bearers of the images of the gods) had to know the other six, which were medical, "treating the constitution of the body, maladies, organs, remedies, the eyes, and questions relating to women."[21]

None of these texts have come down to us. The presence of medical writings is especially interesting in view of the fact that Thoth was known for his medical activity: this could have suggested that Isis should have used him to help resuscitate Osiris. When Thoth also became an astrologer, namely at the time when astrology came into vogue in Egypt, books on this science were attributed to him, and not just medical ones.[22] Lastly, the idea that the god was the author of books may have favored his slide from divine stature to that of historical personage. A twelfth-century text[23] attributes to him a *Golden Bough* and a treatise on the astrolabe, while in the Renaissance the astrolabe is often given him as an attribute.[24]

At the same time, he did not only teach astrology and alchemy, but also magic, which uses material supports such as the statues described in the *Asclepius*, or stones and metals. The borderline between the god Mercury and Trismegistus is not clear here, either, whether regarding the attribution of texts or that of seals and talismans. One Medieval treatise that exists in several manuscripts is ascribed sometimes to Hermes, sometimes to Enoch: it is the *Liber hermetis de quindecim stellis, tot lapidibus, tot herbis, et totidem figuris*, which contains a repertory of images for engraving on stones. Guillaume d'Auvergne and Albertus Magnus were well up in these practices, and helped to make them known.

Documents of this kind were frequently printed in the Renaissance. Giovanni da Fontana, circa 1540, gives among the names to be engraved those of Hermes, Enoch, Tot, Aaron, and Evax. The *Naturae Liber* (Frankfurt, 1625), teaches how to inscribe seals and characters, with therapeutic intention, and shows what are the signs of Hermes, Thetel, and Chael. Among many astrological seals and images, Leo Allatius in *Ars magica sive magis naturalis* (Frankfurt, 1631) gives those of Hermes, Chael, Thetel, and Solomon; a similarly intentioned work is the *Mirabilium* of Rudolf Göckel or Glocenius (1572–1621).[25] In these talismanic repertories, Hermes finds himself associated with entities of which many have a purely magical function. In the next section we will see how Hermes the magus also operates by means of statues.

II. Scenarios and Tablets, or Secrets of the Tomb of Hermes

A. Statues and Cities of Hermes
The long speech of Hermes in the *Asclepius* about the Egyptian statues has caused much ink to flow, irritating Saint Augustine and even upsetting the hermetically inclined authors of the Renais-

sance. It seems to reflect a widespread practice or belief of the Alexandrian domain,[26] to which Michael Maier makes an interesting allusion in his *Symbola aureae mensae*:

> Among other statues [of Hermes], there was a stone one at Achaia Pharis, which gave out oracles. In the evening, they would light incense on its altar, filling the lamps with oil, and place money in the right hand of this statue, then murmur prayers into the ear of the god. These rites completed, the querents would disperse, leaving the temple, and go home with their ears blocked. Then they would go to the market place and unblock their ears, whereupon the first word they heard was to be interpreted as a response from Mercury.[27]

But which one? The god Mercury, or Trismegistus? Maier, although he saw this as an example of superstition, still felt the need of including it in his chapter devoted to the Triplex. Hermetic imagery found the opportunity in such vacillations of expanding in the form of strange pictures constellated around our key-figure. They show him as the founder of a city, or associate him with the discovery of documents containing ineffable revelations. Considered as *urbis conditor*, Mercury-Thoth is the object of an inspired page of that celebrated medieval text, the *Picatrix*, which makes a fairly confused assemblage of more or less vanished traditions. The Arabic original seems to date from the tenth century, the Latin translation used here, from 1256:

> [According to the Chaldeans] Hermes was the first who constructed images by means of which he knew how to regulate the Nile against the motion of the moon. This man also built a temple to the Sun, and he knew how to hide himself from all so that no one could see him, although he was within it. It was he, too, who in the east of Egypt constructed a City twelve miles long within which he constructed a castle which had four gates in each of its four parts. On the eastern gate he placed the form of an Eagle; on

the western gate, the form of a Bull; on the southern gate the form of a Lion, and on the northern gate he constructed the form of a Dog. Into these images he introduced spirits which spoke with voices, nor could anyone enter the gates of the City except by their permission. There he planted trees in the midst of which was a great tree which bore the fruit of all generation. On the summit of the castle he caused to be raised a tower thirty cubits high on the top of which he ordered to be placed a light-house the color of which changed every day until the seventh day after which it returned to the first color, and so the City was illuminated with these colors. Near the City there was abundance of waters in which dwelt many kinds of fish. Around the circumference of the City he placed engraved images and ordered them in such a manner that by their virtue the inhabitants were made virtuous and withdrawn from all wickedness and harm. The name of the City was Adocentyn.[28]

Hermes figures here as a benevolent priest, philosopher, and magician. Our ignorance of the epoch at which the author of *Picatrix* imagined Adocentyn to have been built only serves to increase the seductive and mysterious aspects of his description.

B. The *Book of Crates* and the *Emerald Tablet*

Just as interesting as these statues and cities, and much more numerous, are the scenarios in which someone discovers tablets containing theosophical, astrological, or alchemical revelations. This theme of the revelation of a book or a stele by fortuitous discovery is widespread in the literature of all lands. The revelation may take place in the course of a dream or ecstastic state, or an encounter with a god, or through a sign from heaven. But the name of Hermes is more often linked to the kind obtained from discovering an old book, hidden like a treasure. In the alchemical literature, Bolos the Democritean's speech on the evocation of Ostanes contains the scene in which a column of the temple opens to reveal a book. This topos flourished in the Syriac, and even more in the

Arabic, alchemical writings. Especially popular among the Arabs was the discovery of the document in a tomb: thus the first Hermes, who lived before the Deluge and foresaw it, built the pyramids in order to deposit the secrets of science there before the world was destroyed. This is how the Pseudo-Manetho makes the gnosis go back to the books which he has found in the adyta of the Egyptian sanctuaries where the second Hermes, father of Tat, hid them after writing them. In the *Kore Kosmou*, Hermes, before returning to heaven, engraved and hid his teachings, "so that every generation born after the world would have to search for them." One of the first Arabic texts of this genre, the *Book of Crates*, which dates at the earliest from the sixth century, is fairly typical. The influence of that Arabic literature on Medieval Latin Hermeticism persuades me to include this extract from it:

> I suddenly felt myself swept up into the air, following the same path as the sun and the moon. Then I saw in my hand a parchment entitled . . . : *That which repels the darkness and makes the light to shine.* On this parchment were drawn figures representing the seven heavens, the image of the two great shining stars, and the five wandering planets which follow a contrary path. Each heaven was surrounded by a legend written in stars.
>
> Then I saw an ancient one, the most comely of men, seated at a lectern; he was clothed with white raiment and held in his hand a board of the lectern, on which was placed a book. In front of him were wonderful vessels, the most marvelous I had ever seen. When I asked who this ancient one was, I was told: "He is Hermes Trismegistus, and the book that is before him is one of those that contains the explanation of secrets that he has hidden from men. Remember well all that you see, and retain all that you read or hear, to describe it to your fellow men after you. But do not go beyond what you will be commanded . . . "
>
> Here is what was there, first of all: figures of circles, around which there were inscriptions . . .
>
> When I had finished examining these figures and had grasped

their secret qualities, I leaned over to read what was contained in
the book which Hermes held in his hand.[29]

Settling in Egypt from 640 onwards, the Arabs found manuscripts
and inscribed tablets in the pyramids. The Arabic manuscripts
mention the edifice Abou Hermes at Memphis, in which Hermes
(the father of Thoth!) was reputedly buried; it comprised two
pyramids, one for him and one for his wife.[30] In the tenth century,
all the conditions were therefore present for the elaboration of tales
of the discovery of a tablet of instruction in a tomb of Hermes, while
at the same time alchemy had become fashionable among the
Arabs. One of these revelations is called *The Treasure of Alexander*:
an Arabic treatise on astrology and alchemy, it also contains
reflections on the microcosm and the macrocosm, talismans, and
mentions Hermes as well as Apollonius of Tyana.[31]

The short but very celebrated text of the *Emerald Tablet* belongs
to this literature. Compared to the long narrative of *The Treasure
of Alexander*, its brevity makes it seem, in Julius Ruska's words,
like "a grain of sand beside a mountain."[32] It was E. J. Holmyard
who discovered the oldest known version, which dates from the
eighth century: it was inserted in a text of the Arab Geber, called
The Elementary Book of Foundation, which was certainly translated from the Greek. Without presenting a full scenario, this
mentions Balinus, i.e., Apollonius of Tyana, as having discovered
an engraved tablet in the hand of Hermes.[33] Thus it is the first
known document which mentions an inscription on an emerald
tablet, found in a tomb of Hermes. Apollonius's appearance in this
kind of story is almost natural: he had long been familiar through
the account of his life by Philostratus (170–230 CE), which was
widely distributed—in which, however, there was no mention of
Hermes. The stories of this thaumaturge, a rival to Trismegistus in
the Hermetic imagination, are largely set in Syria. The idea of
placing the tomb of Hermes at Tyana and of having Apollonius
discover Hermetic texts there, as happens in several of these
narratives, could only have occurred after all precise historical

knowledge of him had vanished.[34]

We also find the text of the *Emerald Tablet* as the fourth part of another Arabic writing that can scarcely date from before the twelfth century, attributed to the Christian priest Sagijus, a fictitious character. Sagijus's text begins thus:

> This is what the priest Sagijus of Nabulus dictated on the subject of Balinas's entry into the dark chamber. He said: "I found the following precepts of wisdom at the end of the book of Balinas the Wise: 'When I had penetrated into the chamber above which the talisman was placed, I went forward until I reached an ancient man, seated on a golden throne and holding a tablet of emerald in his hand. It was written in Syriac, in the original language, and it read: [here follows the text of the *Emerald Tablet*].' And such was the plan of Hermes, on whom be the threefold grace of Wisdom."[35]

Syriac was then regarded as the primordial language of mankind, so that if Hermes was supposed to have lived before the Deluge, of course he would have used it! Quite different from the preceding version, this one is almost identical to the one which we have in the Latin translation of Hugo Sanctalliensis, done in the twelfth century. Only the preamble varies substantially. From Hugo's text we learn that Hermes buried these secrets to keep them away from those of insufficient learning, and erected a statue above them. Incidentally, if emerald is again in question here, it is because that was one of the traditional attributes of Hermes, along with quicksiver—just as iron and hematite were ascribed to Mars, lead and black stones to Saturn.[36]

C. The *Liber de Causis* and other Scenarios

Apollonius and Hermes return to the scene together in the *Book of Causes of Apollonius the Wise*, otherwise called the *Book of the Secrets of Creation*. Written at the latest in 750, and at the earliest in the sixth century, it must have been known to Geber. The copy of 1266 contains a third Arabic version of the *Emerald Tablet*.

Another copy, the oldest, dates from 934. Its introductory scenario closely resembles that of *Crates*, but now transported onto Egyptian soil. Here is an extract from it, in which the speaker is Apollonius:

> I will now make known to you my ancestry and my origins. In my native land I was an orphan, and lived in a town called Tuwana. I was destitute. Now there was there a stone statue upon a golden column, on which was written: "Behold! I am Hermes, he who is threefold in Wisdom. I once placed all these marvelous signs openly before all eyes; but now I have veiled them by my Wisdom, so that none should attain them unless he be a sage like myself." On the breast of the statue, one could read in the original language (Syriac): "Let him who would learn and know the secrets of creation and of nature look beneath my foot." But none could understand what this signified: they would look under his foot, and find nothing there.
>
> I was still young and timid; but when my spiritual nature became stronger, I read what was written on the breast of the statue, reflected on what this might mean, and started to dig beneath the plinth. And behold, I came into an underground chamber, so dark that not a single ray of sunlight could penetrate it, though the sun was right overhead, and in which winds arose and blew without ceasing. . . . Because of the darkness I could go no further, and no torch could burn in these winds. I was impotent and gnawed by chagrin; I could not sleep while my heart was so full of care and worry about the difficulties into which I had brought myself.
>
> It was then that an old man appeared, resembling myself in build and appearance. He said to me "O Balinus! Rise, and enter into this chamber to gain knowledge of the secrets of creation, so as to obtain a representation of nature!" I replied: "I can see nothing in that darkness, and the winds that blow there put out every flame." Then he said to me: "O Balinus! Put your light into a glass vessel . . . " I said: "Who are you that allows me to profit

from your favor?" He said to me: "I am your own being, perfect and subtle." Then I awoke full of joy, set a light inside a glass just as my spiritual being had told me to, and entered the chamber. And there I found an ancient man seated on a golden throne, holding in his hand an emerald tablet on which was written: "This is the secret of the world and the knowledge of nature." And before him was a book on which one could read: "This is the secret of the creation, and the knowledge of the causes of things."[37]

New tales began to flower forth in the Middle Ages. One might mention the romance of Perceval, in which the hermit called Trevizrent (i.e., "triple science") is the revealer of the Graal history. Here, incidentally, there is also a reference to a reliquary "green as grass," hence the color of emerald. We should also draw attention to the work of two American scholars, Henri and Renée Kahane, who derive the word "Graal" from the Greek *krater* ("bowl"), in reference to the Bowl of Hermes which appears in the *Corpus Hermeticum*. A text attributed by esoteric tradition to Saint Thomas Aquinas, and cited by Michael Maier, recounts how Abel, the son of Adam, wrote about the virtues and properties of the planets, but was well aware that the Deluge would happen, and so was careful to engrave his teachings on stones. Several centuries after Noah, these stones passed to Mercury Trismegistus—then to Saint Thomas himself, who used them to draw up talismans.[38] Maier's book, recalling the existence of a *Liber de secretis chymicis* attributed to Albertus Magnus, states that Alexander the Great, when visiting the Oracle of Ammon, discovered a tomb of Hermes containing a *tabula Zaradi*, that is, "smaragdine" or emerald. The story had already appeared in Jerome Torella, in a book published in 1496 that deals with astrological images.

Another text, known only through the copy of it made in the seventeenth century, pretends to be a *"Commentary by Toz Graecus, philosopher of great renown, on the books given by Solomon to Rehoboam concerning the Secret of Secrets."* The preface reveals that Solomon gathered his vast learning into a book intended for his son Rehoboam, which he locked up in an ivory coffer concealed in his tomb. Later Toz (Thoth) discovered it, and as he was weeping for his incapacity to understand its contents, an angel of the Lord came to reveal its meaning to him, but enjoined him not to disclose it to any but those who were worthy of it.[39] We also learn, thanks to the *Liber de secretissimo philosophorum opere chemico* (fifteenth century) that Hermes traveled to the Valley of Hebron, where Adam was buried, and there found seven tablets of stone written before the Deluge, containing the doctrine of the Seven Liberal Arts. And the title of a Latin treatise *On the Quintessence*, published in 1460/1476, announces that the latter was given to "Hermes, the prophet and king of Egypt, father of the philosophers, after Noah's flood and by the revelation of an angel sent to him by God."[40]

Of course, these echoes often serve simply for stylistic purposes, obligatory as subtitles or decorative elements that proclaim the nature of the genre. In the eighteenth century, the alchemist Naxagoras says that "a plaque of precious emerald" engraved with inscriptions was made for Hermes Trismegistus after his death, and discovered in his tomb by a woman named Zora, in the Valley of Hebron.[41] Naxagoras, who had read this somewhere or other, makes this kind of detail proliferate as he pleases. His confrère, Hermann Fictuld, found it enough to invent a fiction solely for the sake of setting up a décor: one of his books opens with a scene representing Hermes, an Egyptian priest, strolling between the Elysian Fields and the great World Ocean: accessories which frame a long dialogue inspired by the *Turba philosophorum* and by Maier's *Symbola aureae*.[42]

III. The Beacon of Hermes, or Avatars of the Tradition

A. *Philosophia perennis*

Thanks to the rich variety of his attributes and to his intermediary position betweeen myth and the mythic, Hermes Trismegistus fulfilled all the conditions necessary for becoming an axial personality of a philosophical history of the human race. Strabo already said of Mercury that he gave laws to the Egyptians, and taught philosophy and astronomy to the priest of Thebes, while Marcus Manilius went so far as to see in him the founder of the Egyptian religion. These were bold visions, to be taken up again by Dom Pernéty in the eighteenth century.[43] The most daring chronologies are sometimes the most interesting ones. We cite two of them. According to Roger Bacon, intellectual history began with a plenary divine revelation, of which the Patriarchs were the beneficiaries. The knowledge thus acquired declined because of the sins of humanity, the invention of magic by Zoroaster, and the corruption of wisdom in the hands of Nimrod, Atlas, Prometheus, Aesculapius, Apollo—and Hermes Trismegistus. Bacon is a noteworthy exception in the gallery of guardians of a tradition in which Trismegistus holds a dominant place. He goes on to say that wisdom, restored with Solomon, suffered a new decline that lasted until Thales and Aristotle put philosophy back on its feet again.[44]

A very elaborate historical vision was offered by Scribonius, writing in Marburg in 1583. He states that one should distinguish four schools of physics, i.e., of natural philosophy—a curious theory that resembles that of the four monarchies held by the historiographers of his time. Scribonius names: (A) The Assyrian School, founded by Adam, emphasizing astronomy, astrology, and the interpretation of dreams, and including Noah, Abraham, Moses, David, and Solomon. (B) The Egyptian School, taught by Abraham, in which Hermes and the Persian Magi flourished. They were concerned with natural magic, and invented the division of the day into twelve hours, following the urination of the sacred animals. (C) The Greek School, in which he includes the Druids, the Brahmins and Gymnosophists of India, and also the astrologers and magicians of Scribonius's time who, if one is to believe the Portuguese voyagers, could still enter at will into communication with discarnate entities. (D) The Roman or Latin School, with Cicero and physicians such as Vesalius.[45]

There are also lists of what are called the "sectaries" of Trismegistus. Maier, in *Symbola aureae*, offers us his own version:

Mena, king of Egypt, whose tutor was Hermes Trismegistus; Busiris, who founded Heliopolis; Sesostris, who raised the great statues at Memphis in the Temple of Vulcan; Sethon, in the 3228th year of the world; Adfar Alexandrinus, who taught the art of alchemy to Morienus (an allusion to the text of 1144, cited above); lastly, Calid the Saracen, an Egyptian who was the pupil of Morienus.

There is further the notion of "tradition," more specific than the foregoing testimonies would give one to suppose, but still suggested by them, whose adherents claimed authority in the Renaissance. This term "Tradition," much in vogue today, has been current since the last century, and increasingly so since René Guénon adopted it in the first half of our own. Its underlying idea contains a history that has yet to be written. It seems that the need to conceptualize "Tradition" was felt in the sixteenth century, when it went under the name of *philosophia perennis*; and that it was Agostino Steuco, long before Leibniz, who explained with relative clarity what it consists of.[46] Now, it is a remarkable thing that at the very moment it appeared, the name of Trismegistus was inseparably linked to it. Pico della Mirandola and Marsilio Ficino prepared the way for Steuco, who called our Mercury the "first theologian," and had him succeeded by Orpheus, who then initiated Aglaophemus into his teachings. Then followed Pythagoras, whose disciple was Philolaus, the master of the divine Plato—in whom culminated a *prisca theologia* that began with Mercury. The typical list, being the common denominator of a very large number of those proposed in the course of the sixteenth century and at the beginning of the seventeenth, seems to go as follows: Enoch, Abraham, Noah, Zoroaster, Moses, Hermes Trismegistus, the Brahmins, the Druids, David, Orpheus, Pythagoras, Plato, and the Sibyls.[47] Among several authors with interesting views on the subject, we single out that of Symphorien Champier. The chain of transmission varies somewhat from one of his works to another, but generally one finds, in order: Hermes Trismegistus, Asclepius, Zoroaster, Orpheus, Musaeus, Abraham, Moses, Daedalus, Homer, Lycurgus, Solon, Heraclitus, Plato, Aristotle, Pythagoras, Eudoxus,

Democritus, the Magi, the Gymnosophists, the Hebrew Prophets, the Sibyls, the Druids, Plotinus, Numenius, Philo, and Augustine.[48]

Not the least curious aspect of this version of the Western tradition is its pervasive confusion of the mythological with the real. The need for this distinction had not, in fact, yet been felt, whereas it was thought very important to affirm the existence of an intellectual and spiritual tradition that was unique, or at least relatively homogeneous.

B. Hermeticism and Esotericism

This need for a chain of authorities manifested most notably at the very same moment as the emergence of what would later be called esotericism, i.e., towards the end of the fifteenth century. The discovery of the Jewish Kabbalah, especially after the Diaspora of 1492, was one of the major events after which this esotericism lost no time in taking on its specific form. The other one is the rediscovery of the *Corpus Hermeticum*, brought to Florence in about 1460 by Leonardo da Pistoia, a monk returning from Macedonia. The Middle Ages had not known of it, though they did have the *Asclepius*. Ficino translated the *Corpus* almost in its entirety; it was published in 1471, and had no fewer than sixteen editions before the end of the sixteenth century, not counting partial ones. Before its discovery, Ficino had conceived the ambition of translating Plato: the insistence of Cosimo de' Medici that he set the Platonic texts temporarily aside, those of the *Corpus* being considered more urgent, is some indication of the tenor of the times.

Pico della Mirandola, living in the same Florentine circles, joined to the "magical" philosophy of the Renaissance a Kabbalah which would become more and more Christian; having discovered the Trismegistian *Corpus* through Ficino, he allied it with this Kabbalah through the basic theme of Creation through the Word. This was a marriage with weighty consequences for the evolution of Western esotericism, for this union would give birth to what Frances A.

Yates called a "Hermetico-Kabbalistic tradition" of twofold character: on the one hand theosophic, that is to say, here, speculative and neo-Pythagorean; on the other, magical, and more theurgical than in Ficino.

In the Renaissance, commentaries on the *Corpus Hermeticum* and texts inspired by it are virtually innumerable. Some authors or publishers attributed to Trismegistus texts and teachings that did not even come from the Alexandrian milieu. The Middle Ages had already practised this kind of amalgam, but now it took on different forms. Texts of iatro-mathematics, for example, were often published under the signature of Trismegistus. Conversely, certain commentators struck out passages that did not please them, calling them interpolations. This was especially the case with the *Asclepius*, which contained passages of magical content, particularly the one about statues, that had already scandalized Saint Augustine. Symphorien Champier, acting as the interpreter of many authors, attributed to Apuleius, or even to Geber, the texts that shocked him by being too theurgical. It was in fact precisely in the periods when Hermetic magic was represented as infamous, e.g., in the Latin countries during the Renaissance, that Hermes Trismegistus was made Apollonian.

This "Apollonization" of Trismegistus could be seen as an important trait of the imagination of the epoch. It occurs in exemplary fashion in the collection titled *Champ Fleury*, where the author, on the authority of Boccaccio, makes Mercury the messenger of Light (Jupiter). Mercury comes to rescue Io (Letters) from the prison of Argus (Night), the servant of Juno (Wealth), thus putting back into circulation a knowledge that has been blocked by the guardians of the established intellectual order (Argus), and abolishing fruitless hoarding. Thus Mercury represents the new spirit of Humanism.[49] In the same epoch, one can see even in Ficino how Mercury annexes the figure of Saturn and presents himself in the form of a wise old man, bearded like Moses, thereupon identifying himself with Trismegistus! The fortunes of the latter profited greatly in the Renaissance from the general enthusiasm for the god

Mercury. Gilbert Durand has enumerated seven appearances of this enthusiasm, or this event, the last of them occurring in the nineteenth century.[50] Certainly, the sixteenth century saw Hermes enter the cultural imagination forcibly under his two forms, Mercury and Trismegistus, to the point of serving as a catch-all for a number of derived forms.

Despite reticence with regard to magic, linked in the Latin lands to this form of Apollonism described above, one often sees the *Corpus Hermeticum* accepted as a whole.[51] A prelate like Foix de Candale, author of a very lengthy commentary on it in 1579, regrets that these texts translated by Ficino are not canonical, and suggests that they might deserve to be so. But he piously passes over the magical passages of the *Asclepius*. At the end of the century, Francesco Patrizi tried to convince the pope to have this Hermetic Platonism taught in all Christian schools. Finally, one of the most striking traits of this influence of Trismegistus in the Renaissance is his irenic aspect: in the circles where Hermes passes, one can be sure that tolerance reigns.

C. Resistances and Permanencies

The extreme importance attaching to the idea of a *prisca philosophia* presented a certain danger from the outset, in that it made the authority of a text depend for validation on its antiquity. In 1614, the inevitable happened—and it is astonishing that it happened so late—when a Genevan Protestant, Isaac Casaubon, discovered and proved that these Trismegistic texts were no earlier than the first centuries of the Christian Era. Casaubon did not ask himself whether the error he had uncovered had not proved itself, in the end, a fruitful one: such was not his intention. Some authors deliberately ignored his discovery. Others, at least in the years immediately following, were simply not aware of it. But the result was that these books of Hermes, because they were now known to be far less ancient than had been believed, ceased to command the veneration of as many people as they had done in the past. This disaffection was however a relative one, being amply compensated at the very same moment by the appearance or development of groups and doctrines that would henceforth occupy the vacant place, as it were: Rosicrucianism, and the creation of a Germanic theosophy. One contributory factor in these movements was the slight degree to which Hermeticism had penetrated German thought in the sixteenth century, thanks to the very nature of Lutheranism which stood in the way of Humanism, hence of all that came from the Hellenistic world.

This is not the place to recount the history of Hermetism, let alone of Hermeticism, in modern times, which would involve both its influence and the oppositions it encountered. Let us mention only two tardy and curious examples, which seem to illustrate the theme of this essay. In 1684, Kriegsmann, an author who otherwise distinguished himself with a commentary on the *Emerald Tablet,* published at Tübingen a work entitled *Conjectures on the origin of the German people, and their founder Hermes Trismegistus, who is Chanaan to Moses, Tuitus to Tacitus, and Mercury to the Gentiles.*[52] He studies at length the evidences of Antiquity concerning Ascenates, Tuiton, the Phoenician Taaut, the Egyptian Thoth, and other names. His conclusion is that a Phoenician colony came to Europe, led by Tuiton, i.e. Chanaan and Mercury Trismegistus, or by his son Mannus, and deduces that our Mercury was the founder of Germany.

A little later, in 1700, the Jesuit Joachim Bouvet, a mathematician and musician, was corresponding with Leibniz about the *I Ching.* This Chinese document, wrote Bouvet, is in accordance with "the most admirable remains we have of the wisdom of the Ancients." And this is how Bouvet links up with the idea of tradition:

[It comes] from the same source, and [represents] as precious a remains from the debris of the most ancient and excellent Philosophy, taught by the first Patriarchs of the world to their descendants, then corrupted and almost entirely obscured by the course of time . . . The diagram of Fo-Hi's system was as it were a universal symbol, invented by some extraordinary genius of Antiquity, like Mercury Trismegistus, to represent visually the most abstract principles of all the sciences.[53]

For Bouvet, Fo-Hi was not only a representative of the ancient theology: he actually was Zoroaster, Hermes, or most probably Enoch, and he lived before Moses. Knowing the universal system of this ancient and divine magic would allow us not only to possess the religion of the first patriarchs, but also the ancient and universal system of the sciences. Fo-Hi is the same as Enoch, who is the same as Hermes Trismegistus, and both are prototypes of Christ. Enoch/Fo-Hi/Hermes taught the mathematical symbols of the *I Ching*, but only to men endowed with superior intelligence.[54]

Not long after, Michael de Ramsay, in his *Voyages de Cyrus* (1727), has his protagonist Cyrus encounter our hero in a scenario as inspired as Bouvet's, with many picturesque touches added. After having conversed with the pagan theologians of Antiquity, beginning in Persia with Zoroaster—who preaches the Newtonian doctrine of the ether—Cyrus travels to Thebes, where he undergoes instruction by a pontiff. The latter says: "To make known to you the origin of our religion, our symbols, and our mysteries, you must hear the history of Hermes Trismegistus who founded them. Siphoas, or the second Hermes of this name, was of the race of our first sovereigns." Pregnant with him, his mother was shipwrecked, gave birth on a desert island, and died. "A young goat answered his cries, and fed him with its milk until he grew out of infancy." Thus he passed his early years browsing and eating dates. When the goat died of old age, Hermes had the revelation of life and death: it was then that the First Hermes, or Mercury, appeared to him, taught him, and gave him the name of Trismegistus. Later he concealed the mysteries of religion, the teachings that he had received from the First Mercury, in hieroglyphs and allegories.

The fable of the shipwreck and the goat, somewhat allied to that of "Hai Ibn Yoqdan, the Self-Taught Philosopher" whose history was popular at this period,[55] seems to have been intended to introduce the moral of the story: Cyrus understood, says Ramsay, that the mythologies of the Egyptians and the Persians were founded on the same principles, for "they were merely different names for expressing the same ideas."[56] One also notes the bucolic aspect of this description, inspired by the myth of Hermes-Mercury's birth. Before Ramsay, up to the Renaissance and even afterwards, it was customary to be more prudent in treating mythological subjects, probably because belief was stronger in the tales handed down by tradition.

But beyond its conciliatory and irenical aspect, this passage contains a symbolism worth reflecting on. One thinks of another goat: Amalthea, who nursed Zeus, one of whose horns became the Horn of Plenty. This animal, or the ibex, is the one which mounts highest and can get a foothold on the utmost peaks. Now, island and mountain are traditionally isomorphic, and it is on an island that the story is set. We know, too, that the Tarot relates Jupiter to Hermes, for if Arcanum IV is connected to the former, Arcanum V, the Pope, is reminiscent of the latter. The so-called "papal cross" shown on the Fifth Arcanum, with three horizontal bars intersected by a vertical one, is not without resonances of the symbolism of Fo-Hi, in which Bouvet and Leibniz were interested. Finally, the two axial columns of this Arcanum evoke not only the caduceus, but also, by their verticality, the statue-columns of certain tombs of Hermes as described in legends.[57]

* * *

At the dawn of the Enlightenment, Bouvet and Ramsay were not the only ones to testify to the presence of Trismegistus, despite the intervention of Casaubon. It had been realized, meanwhile, that the dating of the *Corpus Hermeticum* was after all of only relative importance, and entirely secondary to the content of the work—a view eloquently defended by Ralph Cudworth, the Cambridge Neoplatonist.[58] This rather mixed assemblage of inspired texts has always had its hermeneutists, and the eclipses it has undergone since the Renaissance have each been followed by a revival of interest. One of the latter was aided by the vogue of Egyptomania in the eighteenth century, but that alone does not serve to explain it, particularly since Hermes then assumed the role of Isis and

Osiris in their functions of veiling and unveiling. Nowadays, exclusively scholarly works, such as those of Festugière, have not exercised the demythologizing function one might have feared, or hoped for (according to one's preferences): our contemporary esotericists read them with as much fervor as the commentaries that Anglo-Saxon Theosophists of the end of the nineteenth and the beginning of the twentieth century devoted to these same Hermetic texts.

Trismegistus's fortunes have not depended on historical records, any more than the philosophical value of the *Corpus Hermeticum* depended on its age. No one worries about his birth certificate, whether he is identical to Mercury, the brother of that god, an Egyptian priest contemporary with Moses, an Alexandrian philosopher, or what not. A tenacious hypostasis of the god Hermes, he holds an ambiguous place between mythology and historical myth, as well as a favored position in the list of representatives of the *philosophia perennis*: the fact that authors often repeat and recopy the same list, with few variations, can be interpreted as new manifestations of Hermes. Thus when Ficino, Lazarelli, Champier, or Maier mention him in this traditional succession, it is always his presence that actualizes it, as it had done in the Alexandrian writings, simply under a different form. Generally he is present wherever the Western tradition speaks *ex officio*; and even when it does not even mention his name, we suspect that he is present implicitly: we have the impression that he might have been mentioned, for he is the signbearer of this tradition, its marker and beacon—to use the Celtic etymology that Court de Gébelin proposed for the Latin name of Hermes, in which he heard *merc* ("sign") and *cur* ("man").

Hermes Trismegistus obviously possesses several of the essential attributes of this god Hermes: mobility, mutability (eclecticism), discourse and interpretation (hermeneutics), the function of crossroads (tolerance, irenicism). Most important, it seems, is this role of the middle term, held by both figures: Mercury holds the equilibrium between Apollo and Dionysus, while Trismegistus is a catalyst for the union of reason and inspiration, the *logos* and the Sibyls,[59] history and myth. Omnipresent in certain circles such as the Florentine Academy, he does not even have to appear by name: one can sense his spirit in Botticelli's *Primavera*, at the crossroads of mythologizing academicism and the heights of esoteric inspiration, or in a Ficinian talisman. Like Hermes-Mercury, he runs between various currents, linking the separate, skimming over oppositions while stealing their substance, so as to get the Chariot moving, which is the Seventh Arcanum of the Tarot. He is *medicurrius* or *medius currens*, as Saint Augustine and Servius said, while suggesting their own interpretations as given above, hence "he who runs between two" or "in the middle": a fluid place, occupied by an ungraspable personage. But he is not a kind of quicksand or devourer, nor a figure of pure fiction like the masonic Hiram, whose role is merely to function inside a narrative (but with whom he has sometimes been identified).[60] As the place of theosophic, astrological, and alchemical convergences—as the binder of cultural epochs and currents—Trismegistus has been adorned with human and spiritual dimensions according to the requirements of a tradition which he readily symbolizes. Certainly Mercury is more than a messenger—one can see in him a "conductor"—but it is far more to Trismegistus, who is not merely the Medieval pharmacist attentive to the virtues of the peony, that is due the role of "regenerator."[61] The passage from the first to the second, from Olympus to history, corresponds to a fruitful form of reverse euhemerism.

The gods would remain invisible without our aptitude to receive them. Their luminous source passes through various channels, or mirrors, thanks to which they become intelligible to us. The Hermetic works are one of the mirrors of Hermes-Mercury, who signs them as "Hermes-Trismegistus," the figure who holds the armillary sphere.

Notes to Chapter 3

1. Among the most fruitful recent approaches to the idea of literary myth, see Philippe Sellier, "Qu'est-ce qu'un mythe littéraire?" in *Littérature*, no.55 (Paris: Larousse, Oct. 1984), special number entitled *La Farcissure: intertextualités au XVIe siècle*.

2. Among a mass of works of varying inspiration and methodology, one should not omit the following: Charles Ploix, "Hermès," in *Mémoires de la Société linguistique*, vol. II (Paris, 1873), p.22; Laurence Kahar, *Hermès passe, ou les ambiguïtés de la communication* (Paris: Maspero, 1978); Karl Kerényi, *Hermes Guide of Souls: The Mythologem of the Masculine Source of Life*, translated from the German (Dallas: Spring Publications, 1976); Pierre Gordon, *Le Mythe d'Hermès* (Paris: Arma Artis, 1985); Rafael Lopez-Pedraza, *Hermès et ses enfants dans la psychothérapie* (Paris: Imago, 1977); William G. Doty, *Masculinity in Man* (New York: Crossroad, 1993).

3. André-Jean Festugière, *La Révélation d'Hermès Trismégiste*, vol. I: *L'astrologie et les sciences occultes* (Paris: Les Belles Lettres, ed. of 1981), pp.66–88. The reference to Artapan is taken from Eusebius, *Praep. Evang.* IX, 27, 6. Cf. several references in Johann Albrecht Fabricius, *Bibliotheca Graeca* (1705/1728), vol. I, chs. 7–10; also Socrates's statement in Plato, *Phaedrus* 274c–d.

4. Festugière, op. cit., p.78.

5. The most recent presentation, with Greek and French in facing columns, is the best: *Corpus Hermeticum*, text established by A. D. Nock and A.-J. Festugière (Paris: Les Belles Lettres, 4 vols., 1954–1960). The *Asclepius* is contained in vol. IV. Cf. also Festugière's useful summary of the question in his *Hermétisme et gnose païenne* (Paris: Aubier, 1967), pp.28ff. An excellent recent work is Garth Fowden, *The Egyptian Hermes: A Historical Approach to the Late Pagan Mind* (Cambridge University Press, 1986). The *Asclepius* is the Latin adaptation of the *Perfect Discourse*, which is

known thanks to short Greek fragments and to one or two large extracts from a very literal Coptic translation (cf. Jean-Pierre Mahé, *Hermès en Haute-Egypte*, vol. II: *Le fragment du "Discours Parfait" et les définitions hermétiques arméniennes*, Québec: Presses Universitaires de Laval, 1982). On the new Hermetic writings, see Jean-Pierre Mahé, "La voie d'immortalité . . .", pp.347–375 in *Vigiliae Christianae* 45 (1991), which contains a full bibliography. Mahé has written a most informative article on the Hermetica: "La Création dans les Hermetica," pp.3–53, in *Recherches Augustiniennes* (21), 1986. See also, besides vol. II of *Hermès en Haute-Egypte* (cited above), vol. I: *Les textes hermétiques de Nag Hammadi et leurs parallèles grecs et latins*, Québec: Presses Universitaires de Laval, 1978.

6. Festugière, *Hermétisme*, p.30; *La Révélation*, vol. I, p.81.

7. In Coptic treatise "The Eighth Reveals the Ninth" (Codex Nag Hammadi, 6), p.58, lines 4–6, Hermes says: "I am the Intellect and I see another Intellect who sets the soul in motion": here, Hermes identifies himself with the divine Intellect who sets in motion the Soul of the World as well as all the individual souls; cf. also Jean-Pierre Mahé, *Hermès en Haute-Egypte*, vol. I [see n. 5], p.77.

8. Michael Maier, *Symbola aureae mensae duodecim nationum* (Frankfurt, 1617), pp.10f.; facsimile with introduction by Karl R.-H. Frick (Graz: Akademische Druck- und Verlagsanstalt, 1972). But there are abundant examples of the interpretation as "philosopher, priest, and king." Cf. also Françoise Bonardel, *L'Hermétisme* (Paris: P.U.F., 1985, collection "Que sais-je?"), p.14. On the number three, cf. Mirko Sladek, "Mercurius triplex, Mercurius termaximus et les 'trois Hermès'" in *Présence d'Hermès Trismégiste* (Paris: Albin Michel, 1988), pp.88–99.

9. Lynn Thorndike, *History of Magic and Experimental Science*, 7 vols. (New York: Columbia Univ. Press, 1923–1958), vol. II, pp. 219, 253.

10. Festugière, *La Révélation*, vol. I, p.75; *Corpus Hermeticum*, ed. cit. [see n.5], vol. III, pp.clxiii, clix.

11. *Corpus Hermeticum*, vol. II, p.357. St. Augustine, *City of*

God, bk. xviii, chs. 8 [citation given here], 39; bk. vii, ch. 14 (*medius currens*); bk. viii, ch. 26 (reference to *Asclepius*), trans. John Healey (1610). Cf. also Bonardel, *L'Hermétisme* [see n.8], p.57.

12. Edition consulted: Jo. Jacob Manget, *Bibliotheca chemica curiosa* (Geneva, 1702), vol. I, p.509; facsimile ed., Sala Bolognese: A. Forni, 1976. The title of this alchemical text is *Liber de compositione Alchemiae, quem edidit Morienus* (pp.509–519).

13. *Summa Philosophia Roberto Grosseteste ascripta*, ed. L. B. Baur, in *Beiträge zur Geschichte des Mittelalters*, ed. Bäumker, vol. IX (1912), pp.275–643. Cf. pp.275ff.

14. British Library, Ms. Arundel 377, *Philosophia Magistri Danielis de Morlai*, fols.892, 892v. Cited in Thorndike [see n.9], vol. II, p.223.

15. *Hermes Triplex de VI rerum principiis multisque aliis naturalibus, partitusque quinque; cum prologo de tribus Mercuriis.* Also titled: *Hermetis Trismegisti opuscula quaedam: primum de VI rerum principiis.* Cited in Thorndike [see n.9], vol. II, p.223.

16. Cited after the French ed. of 1549 (*Mercure Trismégiste Hermès*, Paris, trans. Gabriel du Préau); original ed., 1507. On Ficino's text, cf. Michael Allen, "Marsile Ficin, Hermès et le Corpus Hermeticum," in *Présence* [see n.8], pp.110–119.

17. *Symbola aureae* [see n.8].

18. *Symbola aureae*, pp.9ff. I have not found this passage in the editions of Palaephastus' book consulted in the Bibliothèque Nationale.

19. F. J. W. Schröder, *Bibliothek für die höhere Naturwissenschaft und Chemie* (Marburg & Leipzig, 1775–1776), vol. I, p.145; Nicholas Lenglet-Dufresnoy, *Histoire de la philosophie hermétique* (Paris, 1742), vol. I, p.10; M. de Ramsay: see n.56.

20. Dom Antoine Joseph Pernéty, *Les Fables égyptiennes et grecques dévoilées et réduites au même principe* (Paris, 1786), vol. I, pp.165, 174, 177 (1st ed., 1758).

21. *Stromata* VI.4, 35ff. Manetho, Selencus, Iamblichus: cf. *Les Mystères d'Egypte* (Paris: Les Belles Lettres, 1966), p.195.

22. Festugière, *La Révélation* [see n.3], p.125.

23. Cited in n.15. Cf. Thorndike [see n.9], vol. II, p.223.

24. Cf., for example, the title page and p.5 of *Symbola* [see n.8]; also J. Boissard, *De divinatione et magicis praestigiis* (Oppenheim, n.d. [beginning of 17th cent.]), p.140. And Chapter 5 in this book.

25. Cf. numerous references in Thorndike [see n.9], vol. II, pp.220, 228, 247, 254, 258. Leo Allatius wrote on the Art of Memory—to be added to the dossier on the subject by Frances A. Yates.

26. See M. Weynants-Ronday, *Les Statues vivantes: Introduction à l'étude des statues égyptiennes* (Brussels: Fondation égyptologique, 1926); George Maspéro, "Le double et les statues prophétiques," in *Etudes de mythologie et d'archéologie égyptiennes*, vol. I of *Bibliothèque égyptienne* (Paris, 1893), especially pp.82ff.

27. *Symbola aureae* [see n.8], p.19.

28. *Sunt etiam magi qui in hac sciencia et opere se intromiserunt Caldei; hi namque in hac perfectiores habentur sciencia. Ipsi vero asserunt quod Hermes primitus quandam domum ymaginum construxit, ex quibus quantitatem Nili contra Montem Lune agnoscebat; hic autem domum fecit Solis. Et taliter ab hominibus se abscondebat quod nemo secum existens valebat eum videre. Iste vero fuit qui orientalem Egipti edificavit civitatem cuius longitudo duodecim miliariorum consistebat, in qua quidem construxit castrum quod in quatuor eius partibus quatuor habebat portas. In porta vero orientis formam aquile posuit, in porta vero occidentis formam tauri, in meridionali vero formam leonis, et in septentrionali canis formam construxit. In eas quidem spirituales spiritus fecit intrare qui voces proiciendo loquebantur; nec aliquis ipsius portas valebat intrare nisi eorum mandato. Ibique quasdam arbores plantavit, in quarum medio magna consistebat arbor que generacionem plantavit, in quarum medio magna consistebat arbor que generacionem fructuum omnium apportabat. In summitate vero ipsius castri quandam turrim edificari fecit, que triginta cubitorum longitudinem attingebat, in cuius summitate pomum ordinavit rotundum, cuius color qualibet die usque ad septem dies mutabatur. In fine vero septem dierum priorem quem habuerat recipiebat colorem. Illa autem civitas quotidie ipsius mali cooperiebatur colore, et sic civitas predicta qualibet die*

*refulgebat colore. In turris quidem circuitu abundans erat aqua, in
qua quidem plurima genera piscium permanebant. In circuitu
vero civitatis ymagines diversas et quarumlibet manerierum
ordinavit, quarum virtute virtuosi efficiebantur habitantes ibidem
et a turpitudine malisque languoribus nitidi. Predicta vero civitas
Adocentyn vocabatur.*

Arabic text published by H. Ritter: "Picatrix, ein arabisches
Handbuch hellenistischer Magie," in *Studien der Bibliothek
Marburg*, vol. XII (1933). German translation of this Arabic text by
H. Ritter & M. Plessner, in *Studies of the Warburg Institute*, vol.
27 (University of London, 1962). Latin ed. by David Pingree (London: Warburg Institute, 1986): passage cited, pp.188f. I cite the
English translation by Frances A. Yates in her *Giordano Bruno and
the Hermetic Tradition* (London: Routledge & Kegan Paul, 1964),
p.54. Achmounein, or Hermopolis: the first name signifies "eight,"
the number of divinities worshipped in this city. Hermes was
sometimes known there as "Lord of the City of the Eight." Cf.
Mirko Sladek, *Fragmente der hermetischen Philosophie in der
Naturphilosophie der Neuzeit* (Bern: Peter Lang, 1984), p.42.

29. Text in Marcellin Berthelot, *La Chimie au Moyen Age* (Paris:
Steinheil, 1893).

30. *Ibid.*, p.27.

31. Julius Ruska, *Tabula Smaragdina: Ein Beitrag zur Geschichte
der hermetischen Literatur* (Heidelberg: C. Winter, 1926), pp.68–79
(original text and Arabic translation of *The Treasure of Alexander*).

32. Ruska, p.79.

33. Ruska, pp.120ff.

34. Ruska, the entire chapter, which is most illuminating on this
question.

35. Ruska, pp.114f. See also *Aurei Velleris Oder Der Guldin
Schatz-und Kunst-Kammer*, Tractatus III (Rorschach, 1598). Concerning the *Emerald Tablet*, one learns that Hermes lived before
the Deluge and went to the Valley of Hebron, where he found
marble columns on which the Seven Liberal arts were carved. The
scenario in which Hermes is discovered in a tomb or secret

chamber is found again in the Arabic anonymous studied by Ruska in "Studien zu Muhammad Ibn Umail," in *Isis* 22, no. 37, vol. XXIV/1 (Dec. 1935), pp.310–342. This Arabic text was the subject of Latin adaptations and of a fine illustration; cf. plates II, VII, and VIII in the present book, and Barbara Obrist, *Les Débuts de l'imagerie alchimique (XIVe–XVe siècles)* (Paris: Le Sycomore, 1982).

36. Ruska [see n.31], pp.178f.

37. Ruska, pp.138f. This citation is based [by J. Godwin] on Ruska's German translation from the Arabic.

38. *Symbola* [see n.8], p.20; text attributed to St. Thomas: *De Ente et Essentia.*

39. *Symbola*, pp.24f. Jerome Torella, *Opus praeclarum de imaginibus astrologicis* (Valencia, 1496), fol. e.v., recto; cited in Thorndike [see n.9], Vol. IV, p.580.

40. Thorndike, Vol. II, p.219. Text published by Frederick Furnival (London 1886; edition seen, 1889). See also *Aurei Velleris* [see n.35].

41. *Supplementum Aurei Velleris*, pp.11f., in *Aureum Vellus oder Güldenes Vliess* (Frankfurt, 1733).

42. *Turba Philosophorum, das ist: Gesammelte Sprüche der Weisen zur Erläuterung der hermetischen Schmaragd-Tafel* (n.p., 1763); written in 1759.

43. Pernéty [see n.20], pp.172f.

44. *Opus Maius*, ed. J. H. Bridges (London, 1897), vol. I, pp.20, 45f., 65.

45. Guilielmus Adolphus Scribonius, *Rerum naturalium doctrina methodica* (2nd ed., 1583); cf. Scribonius's own letter at the head of the work, dated 1583. Cited in Thorndike [see n.9], vol. VI, p.353.

46. Agostino Steuco, *De perenni philosophia* (Lyon, 1540). Cf. Charles B. Schmitt, "Perennial Philosophy: from Agostino Steuco to Leibniz," in *Journal of the History of Ideas*, vol. XXVII (Jan.–March 1966), pp.505–532.

47. Cf. especially D. P. Walker, *The Ancient Theology: Studies in Christian Platonism from the Fifteenth to the Eighteenth Century* (London: Duckworth, 1972), p.20.

48. Brian P. Copenhaver, *Symphorien Champier and the Reception of the Occultist Tradition in Renaissance France* (The Hague: Mouton, 1978), pp.119f. Almost the same list is found in Lazarelli [see n.16], p.8.

49. Geoffroy Tory, *Champ Fleury, ou l'Art et Science de la Proportion des Lettres Attiques et vulgairement lettres Romaines proportionnées selon le Corps et Visage humain* (Paris, 1526); facsimile, ed. G. Cohen, 1931. See also *supra*, Chapter 1, p.35.

50. Gilbert Durand, "Permanence et dérivations du mythe de Mercure," in *Actes del Colloqui Internacional (1985) sobre els valors heuristica de la Figura d'Hermes*, ed. Alain Verjat in the series "Mythos," of the Grup de Recerca sobre l'Imaginari (Barcelona: Universitat de Barcelona: Facultat de Filologia, 1986), pp.5–27. Cf. the end of Chapter 1 in the present book.

51. Cf. Copenhaver [see n.48], index of names.

52. W. Chr. Kriegsmann, *Conjectaneorum de Germanicae gentis origine, ac Conditore, Hermete Trismegisto, qui S. Moysi est Chanaan, Tacito Tuito, Mercuriusque Gentilibus. Liber unus. Isque in Taciti de Moribus Germanorum Opusculum, diversis locis Commentarius posthumus* (Tübingen, 1684). This author is the same as that of the treatise on the *Emerald Tablet* published by Manget [see n.12].

53. Quoted by Walker [see n.47], p.221.

54. *Ibid.*, pp.224, 226.

55. See Abu Bakr ibn al-Tufail, *Philosophus autodidactus, sive epistola Abi Jaafar Ebn Tophail de Hai Ebn Yokdhan, in qua ostenditur quomodo ex inferiorum contemplatione ad superiorum notitiam ratio humana ascendere possit*, trans. E. Pococke (Oxford, 1671); English trans., London, 1674.

56. *Voyages of Cyrus*, Edition of 1730, pp.120ff., 129ff.

57. I am grateful to Paul-Georges Sansonetti for drawing my attention to this symbolic similarity.

58. Cf. the excellent passage on Cudworth in Ernest Lee Tuveson, *The Avatars of Thrice Great Hermes: An Approach to Romanticism* (London & Toronto: Associated Univ. Presses, 1982), pp.67–

75.

59. On this aspect of Trismegistus, see Bonardel's fine study [see n.8].

60. As an example of this identification, see the masonic ritual of the "Magi of Memphis," in "Zwei Hochgrad-Rituale des 18. Jahrhunderts," translated by Otto Schaaf, published in *Das Freimaurer-Museum. Archiv für freimaurerische Ritualkunde und Geschichtsforschung*, t.IV (Zeulenroda/Leipzig: B. Sporn, 1928), pp.207–245.

61. A comparison borrowed from F. Bonardel, see *supra*, n. 8, p.18.

CHAPTER FOUR

Hermes's Presence in the City

If one tends to find nymphs in grottoes, one can be even more certain of meeting Hermes wherever there are crossroads and intersections, be they as different as those of a conference or of a city. He even seems to wait at the places where one city intersects with another, so as to enter each one under a different guise. Thus we find him in the city of a Hermetic myth: Adocentyn, a fictional town belonging to esoteric tradition; in Amsterdam, a propitious place for initiatic wanderings, in Gustav Meyrink's novel *The Green Face*; in a Mexican suburb, as short of hope as it is of bread, in Luis Buñuel's film *Los Olvivados*; and finally in a fictional setting reflecting contemporary fears and obsessions, in George Miller's *Mad Max Beyond Thunderdome*. Two imaginary cities, two real ones. Two texts, two films. And five Hermeses . . .

Hermes the Architect, or Hermetistic Harmony
Considered as a mythical place, the city of Hermopolis deserves a lengthy study. We know that the local divinity of Khmonou (the modern Achmouein) in Middle Egypt was Thoth, called Hermes by the Greeks and credited with the role of *urbis conditor*, founder of the city. The tradition vacillates between identifying this person-age with the god Hermes and with Hermes Trismegistus, a signifi-cant ambiguity which points to the meeting-place of Myth with History. The reader should refer here to the passage in Chapter 3 (see pages 88–89), translated from the famous Arabic book of magic, the *Picatrix*, whose supposed author Magriti or Madjriti lived in the second half of the tenth century. A Latin translation made in 1256 at the command of King Alphonsus of Castile was widely distrib-uted in Europe.

The rich symbolism of this passage invites an interesting historical and comparative study. The city's fluidity (water), mobile colors (like a science-fiction decor), and therapeutic talismans are so many attributes of Hermes, bestowed on the city which he founded and adorned. To this text I would like to juxtapose a witness to a cultic practice, or rather a form of popular magic, interesting here because of its urban setting. It evokes Hermes within the city, rather than as the god who presided over its conception. We read this in *Symbola aureae mensae duodecim nationum*, a Latin work of Michael Maier, which appeared in Frankfurt in 1617. The reader will find the passage in Chapter 3 of the present book.[1]

It is a lively description, which in few words sketches the whole scene with its several tableaux. The citizens, presumably numerous, cover the distance between the temple and the forum with their fingers in their ears, then mingle with the crowd and await their illumination. This is the image that Maier passed on to his late Renaissance contemporaries. But in the Renaissance itself, there is no lack of Hermes figures connected with the town. Many of them illustrate Hermes's euphemization, his transition to the status of a psychological type or a decorative motif. In his posthumous "Hymn to Hermes," Ronsard places him in the crossroads of the city, where he performs his sleight-of-hand tricks like the Conjuror of the Tarot:

> *Tu es des charlatans le seigneur, et de ceux*
> *Qui des peuples béans amusent autour d'eux*
> *Vendeurs de thériaque, et de ceux qui aux places*
> *Jouants des gobelets font tours de passe-passe*

> You're the lord of all charlatans, and of those
> Amused by the faces that gape all around them;
> Of theriac hawkers, and those in the squares
> Who play with the cups and do conjuring tricks.[2]

I will now take three images from the repertory of our own time, drawn from fiction and the cinema. Here we meet Hermes again, only he is disguised and rechristened.

At the Crossroads of Amsterdam, or the Initiatic Message

One might be tempted to see in the city of Amsterdam, a place of hallucinatory expressionistic density, and in Chidher Green or Hermes, the two principal characters of a marvelous novel by the Austrian writer Gustav Meyrink: *Das Grüne Gesicht* of 1916 (*The Green Face*). Around them gravitate the other personages of the drama, more stereotyped than psychologized, since the essence of the work, as in all traditional stories, is the initiatic pilgrimage. The book opens with the writing on a shop-sign in an Amsterdam street: "Jokes and Tricks, Salon of Chidher Green," and we are very soon plunged into a world of thoroughfares, passages, canals, little shops, and mysterious communications between places as well as people—a labyrinth at whose center is Chidher, invisible or diaphanous, ungraspable and always in disguise. Hauberisser, the neophyte on whom destiny inflicts the trials that make up the novel's plot, believes he has read somewhere the name of this mysterious character, then thinks he was mistaken; he wanders in the city trying to recompose his mind and gather his thoughts:

"All right, Miss, that's enough of that; at least tell me who this Chidher Green is, the one whose name is out there on the sign."

"What sign, please?"

"For heaven's sake, Miss! Outside on the shop-sign!"

The salesgirl opened her eyes wide. "Our shop-sign says Zitter Arpad!" she stammered in amazement.

Hauberisser snatched up his hat and hurried outside to make certain. Mirrored in the glass door, he saw the shopgirl tapping her forehead with a look of astonishment. Once outside, he looked up at the proprietor's sign and read it. His heart nearly stopped beating as he saw that under the words "Jokes and Tricks" there was indeed the name of Zitter Arpad.

Not a letter of "Chidher Green."

He was so confused and felt so ashamed of himself that he left his walking-stick in the shop's rack and hurried straight off, so as to get into another neighborhood as quickly as possible. . . .

For a good hour, he wandered mindlessly through all sorts of streets, coming into deathly quiet lanes and cramped courtyards in which churches would suddenly rise up before him, dreaming in the warm sunlight. He walked through dark doorways, cool as cellars, and heard his steps echo as if in a monastery cloister.

The houses were dead, as if no human being had lived there for centuries. Here and there an angora cat slept among flowerpots garish with color on baroque windowsills, blinking in the golden noontide light; not a sound.

High elm trees with motionless branches and leaves loomed out of tiny green gardens, surrounded by a host of ancient gabled houses which, with their black fronts and bright wood-framed windows, clean as Sunday, seemed to reach towards each other like friendly old matrons.

[Hauberisser finds himself in a medieval part of the city]

Sundials on the walls, above splendid and flowery coats-of-arms, dazzling window-panes, red tiled roofs; little chapels sunk in shadow, and the golden balls on towers shimmering upwards towards chubby white clouds.

A grille stood ajar, leading to a cloistered courtyard. He went in and saw a bench beneath the branches of a weeping willow. Around him was tall, rank grass. Not a soul in sight anywhere; not a face behind the windows. All was still as death.

He sat down to gather his thoughts.[3]

His name is Chidher Green, but also Ahasver; he is "a precursor of primordial man, who knew nothing of death." He wears on his forehead a black headband, under which is hidden the symbol of eternal life.[4] Like Thoth-Hermes, Chidher is connected with Egypt. Someone says that they have seen his portrait in the Museum of Leiden; in fact, this museum does not contain the picture, "but only Egyptian antiquities." The symbol of the scarab reinforces this connection, as does the appearance at the end of the story of Thoth himself in a vision, as a man "with an Ibis head" holding in his hand the Egyptian sign of life: the cross surmounted by a ring, symbol of eternal life. His other name, Ahasver, readily leads one to take him for Ahasuerus, the Wandering Jew: the unhappy man condemned never to die as he expiates over the centuries the sin committed at Golgotha, where he refused to help Jesus carry his cross. He certainly possesses this character's quality of traveler or wanderer; and one also thinks of the immortality attributed to St. John the Evangelist (John 21.20–23). But he is even more evocative of the prophet Elijah, as one character in the novel is careful to remind us: "I knew that he was Elijah, although my wife pretended that he was called Chidher Green." Finally, the color green obviously recalls that of the *Emerald Tablet*, attributed to Hermes Trismegistus.

At the end of the novel, the destruction of the city by a terrific hurricane follows the final revelation that Chidher grants Hauberisser by means of a manuscript which goes back to a very ancient Egyptian fraternity, the Brotherhood of Heliopolis. It is an apocalypse brought about by the element of air, which extends far beyond Amsterdam to take on cosmic dimensions, leaving hope only for the redemption of individuals favored by Chidher-Hermes, the guardian of mysteries and of magic, seeker and gatherer of the elect upon earth. As hierophant, the only truly living man, he awakens to the mystical resurrection, like St. John in the Gnostic legends. Legend come to reality: that is the theme of Meyrink's novels *The Golem, The Green Face,* and *Walpurgis Night.* In each instance it is the city that becomes the place "where the frontier between here and the beyond is thinner than anywhere else."[5] Like Prague, Amsterdam is saturated with culture, history, and an infinitude of memories; in these cities there is a more tenuous frontier than usual between the visible and the invisible.[6] It is a fragile place, whose decomposition was already a theme of Decadent literature, and which culminates in an apocalypse whose prelude presents Hermes as the supreme figure of the Mediator.

Little-Eyes, or the Discreet Presence of Mercury

In chronological order, my third example of the Hermesian figure is that of a Hermes euphemized, discreet in his presence, reduced to a supporting role, and powerless in the midst of misery and desolation while still keeping his traditional attributes. I detected him in a famous film of Luis Buñuel, made in 1950: *Los Olvivados*, which takes us into the sordid world of a Mexico City suburb.[7] It is certainly a realistic film, but its mythical aspects come as no surprise from such a poetic director who, besides, is marked by surrealism. The city here is the centerless and peripheral world of the subproletariat, a world of waste grounds, of garbage dumps where dead babies are sometimes thrown; yet it still has a market where there is a merry-go-round to delight the children, and also meeting places for young hooligans. Shortly after the beginning of the film it is here, at a crossroads and at the foot of a fountain, that a little peasant of twelve or thirteen appears, called Ojitos ("Little-Eyes" in Spanish), dressed in a poncho and straw hat. We soon learn that his father has abandoned him here a few hours earlier, probably for good. One might expect a heroic mission to await him, since this scene evokes the theme of the exposed child, left in this transitory place that is the world with its armed robbers, murderers, and all its perils—an exposure that seems to be symbolized by the fountain—just as the child-heroes of tales and myths are often given to the waters. But there is nothing of this, any more than in the myth of Hermes. Ojitos meets a blind old man who lives by singing and playing crude musical instruments; he helps him cross the street, then serves him as guide and finds onlookers for him. Later one sees him teaching Meche, a girl from a poor family, that to keep from falling sick one should carry a dead man's tooth. He offers Meche the necklace on which is threaded the one he wears, which he himself went to find in a cemetery by moonlight. He also teaches her that to keep one's skin smooth and young-looking, one should rub it with a rag soaked in milk. He serves several times as news-bringer to a gang of children. Still at the crossroads of the market place, it is again Ojitos who tells his friend Pedro that the latter is no longer wanted by the police.

Ojitos thus possesses most of the attributes of Hermes. *Crossroads*: this little vagabond hovers between country and town, having left the one without ever belonging to the other, and hangs about by day at the intersection marked by the fountain in the market place. *Communication*: he is a mediator, however modest, between the world of the dead and that of the living (the allusion to the cemetery), and carries messages. *Games and Shows*: he participates indirectly by helping the blind musician. *Therapeutics and Magic*: he shows a flair for cures, for prolonging youth and life. His status in the film is the very special one of marginal among the marginals, since in the end practically nothing happens to him while all around him are nothing but thefts, violence, and murders—beside some acts of real humanity. When Pedro is killed, Ojitos leaves the story as if he had only passed through it as a temporary guide, and tells Meche simply that he is going off to look for his father again.

Hermes euphemized, like the decorative elements found in certain mythological emblems of the sixteenth to eighteenth centuries, this little Mercury of the slums is brother to the one in Joseph Losey's *Messenger* (1971), but without occupying a lead part. Ojitos remains a supporting role, albeit the most important one. On a higher plane, going beyond the message of the film, he is by far the most interesting character in it precisely because he is enigmatic and traditional, reminding one of the child with the light in Rembrandt's *Night Watch*. That Buñuel does not seem to have intended to be "mythical" makes Ojitos all the more authentically symbolic. Thanks to Hermes as go-between, Myth is discreetly present in the city of desolation.

The Meeting of Two Hermeses in the City of Screaming Metal

We conclude with a more recent work, also a film: *Mad Max Beyond Thunderdome* (1985), the second sequel of the original *Mad Max* (1979), highly successful since its first screening.[8] The historical framework is the same as in its two predecessors: near the former city of Sydney, destroyed—as we know from *Mad Max II* (1981)—along with the rest of the world in a nuclear war. The survivors live among a heterogeneous mess of salvaged objects, instruments turned from their original purposes, constructions out of junk. By showing micro-societies and embryonic towns where people are evolving in the midst of an incredible bric-à-brac, the director George Miller and his designers give full rein to their imaginations as they sketch this new world.

At the beginning of the film, Mad Max, the hero, discovers the little urban settlement of Bartertown. It is a sort of surreal platform for swapping the most varied and improbable sorts of goods, but most of all it is the scene of merciless combats. The locals' regular and favorite spectacle is a fight between two gladiators, of whom one is invariably killed. This show, pitiless and completely amoral, takes place in an improbable transparent structure called the Thunderdome. Here we meet Dr. Dealgood, the master of ceremonies of these combats and Bartertown's auctioneer.[9] He wears a black cape that suggests Dracula more than Hermes, but also a scepter that indicates his hermesian role, for it is tipped by a winged wheel. He is flanked by two girls, which is quite concordant with the trinitary character of Hermesian figures.[10]

Dr. Dealgood is an incredible braggart, whose Word transforms the sordid into a demoniacal beauty; a commentator on the brutal reality, encouraging Evil by the magic of a speech that is wonderfully glib and invisibly effective. He is a degenerate Hermes, a perverted Mercury, "fallen" because he is the spokesman for humans who have usurped the Gods, as appears in his superb harangue before and after the combat in the Thunderdome. The latter stands as the mythical center of the town, presented as an arena with a function comparable to that of ancient Rome. The principles that rule this town do not rest on divine will, but on a double egotistic power. There is the Master, the old dwarf who rules beneath the town in the midst of a herd of pigs—traditional symbol of fecundity—whose excrement is used as a source of energy, just as the gnomes and kobolds of legend are masters of the energies of the earth. The degeneracy is underlined by the equally unchallenged power of "Aunt Entity," the usurper of a sovereignty that is both uranian and lunar, as the silvery scales of her armor and her aerial residence suggest.

But Dr. Dealgood is not the sole Hermes. We see another in the person of Jedediah, the airborne robber who at the start of the film uses his his old plane to surprise Mad Max in the middle of the desert and steal his team of camels—which he will swap for something or other in Bartertown, just as Hermes stole Apollo's herd of cows. Like the god, Jedediah makes his home in a cavern and appears with a child whose weapon recalls the bow of Eros. Above all, this wily and elusive character who is master of the air is devoted to the juncture between past and future. At the end it is he who takes the place of the captain awaited by the surviving youngsters—Captain Walker, whose role he takes on; and he allows the myth to reach total accomplishment and realization, just as Chidher Green, in Meyrink's novel, ensured that of the soteriological and apocalyptic myth. Here the power of the magician-warrior, incarnated by the people of the Fault, reestablishes a society to which Myth is central—the return to the "wasteland," the promised city, former Sydney—as opposed to the society of Bartertown, founded on wheeling and dealing (=capitalism) and brute force (=totalitarianism). Mad Max himself is no Hermes. The role devolves on Dr. Dealgood in its perverted form, and on the robber-pilot under the form of the Trickster, well known to mythologists and ethnologists. This Trickster, as Jedediah, leads the children of the Fault (the paradisal Green Land, as opposed to the "waste" land of the desert) back to the land of their ancestors, the great city destroyed by nuclear war, so as to restore life to the dead city and allow the film to end with a glorious galaxy of lights which, in the last image, shine in the remains of Sydney as if proclaiming a new civilization and a new humanity.

The presence of Hermes has been detected by Jean Lorente in another movie: *Notorious*, by Alfred Hitchcock (1946). In this top-notch espionage tale, Cary Grant is a kind of messenger of the Gods who salvages a girl (Ingrid German) thanks to a trick, takes her to the skies (in a plane, of course). The journey proves to be initiatic and ends up on a new Promised Land. Finally, like Hermes delivering Io from the watching eyes of Argus, the hero delivers the heroine from the prison of a shotgun wedding.[11]

* * *

These very different examples reflect imaginal modes in which the god and the city have linked roles:

(A) Hermes as *urbis conditor*, ruling from the heights the city which he has built and which he links to the cosmos and the archetypal world. Here we are in the realm of Myth. The *Picatrix* does not present itself as a work of fiction: the Arab author believes what he is telling us, and addresses believers. Adocentyn is the model city, utopian (but not in the sense of modern history), oriented to the above. Utopias are projected into the future, not the past, but this city is, like them, static, its structure and symbols conferred on it by the divine image.

(B) Hermes as initiator in the labyrinthine and expressionistic city: without him, Amsterdam would be Kafka-esque, a tangled mass working the decay of its stones and its souls. Thanks to Chidher, the final catastrophe of the hurricane that devastates the city takes on a more metaphorical than real character. Chidher-Hermes is the psychopomp *par excellence*, favoring ruses and disguises. Unlike the preceding example, the author has written a text of explicit fiction, while the mythic figures and the descriptions of the city serve an esoteric teaching: an "orientation"—an Orient—is possible thanks to the deciphering of the signs, helped by the best of guides.

(C) Hermes exiled, lost in the peripheral world of a town without East or West, in an excrescence of the tentacular city with its sprawling suburbs. To my mind, Ojitos is the Hermes who brings the most precious and most original message of all these four works. He seems to tell us that it is up to us to discover the discreet presence of mythological figures beyond the greyness and the misery of our real and figurative cities.

(D) The "transient" Hermeses, degenerate or reduced to the role of tricksters in the multiple and mobile city, moving from Sydney to Bartertown and back again to Sydney. It is the passing from a state of Fall to a Redemption or reintegration: one of the rare examples where the city takes part in a process of metamorphosis based on myth. Bartertown is at the same time the affirmation, or the suspicion, that Myth is the founder of all culture, and that without it, a humanity that has forgotten its lost civilization cannot make a new beginning.

What these four examples have taught us is perhaps a method for reassembling the scattered elements of our dissociated universe, and of reconstituting it. They teach us how to make good use of our Myths.

Notes to Chapter 4

1. See Chapter 3, under "Statues and Cities of Hermes."

2. Quoted by Ludwig Schrader in *Panurge und Hermes: Zum Ursprung eines Charakters bei Rabelais* (Bonn: Romanisches Seminar der Universität Bonn, 1958), p.119.

3. Gustav Meyrink, *Das grüne Gesicht* (Munich: Kurt Wolff Verlag, 1921), pp.133–136.

4. Ibid., p.71.

5. J. J. Pollet, "La ville fantastique de Gustav Meyrink," in *Ecritures de la ville dans les lettres allemandes du XXè siècle* (U.E.R. Etudes Germaniques, Université de Lille III: Presses Universitaires de Valenciennes, 1985, no. 10), p.125.

6. Ibid., pp.127, 131.

7. The script has been published by Claude Beylie, in *L'Avant-Scène* (Paris), no. 137, June 1973.

8. See the interesting file devoted to *Mad Max* in *L'Ecran Fantastique* (Paris), no. 60, September 1985.

9. Ibid., p.51.

10. Gilbert Durand, *Les Structures anthropologiques de l'Imaginaire* (Paris: Bordas, 1969), pp.229ff. (new edition, Dunod, 1985).

11. Jean Lorente, "Hermès au cinéma: *Notorious* d'Alfred Hitchcock mythocritiqué," in *Colloqui International sobre els Valors Herístics de la Figura Mític d'Hermes*. Collective work edited by Alain Verjat, in the series ΜΥΘΟΣ of the Grup de Recerca sobre l'Imaginari i Mitocrítica (Barcelona: Universitat de Barcelona, Facultat de Filologia, 1986. Acts of the Proceedings of the Conference in Barcelona, March 1985), pp.283–285.

CHAPTER FIVE

The Faces of Hermes Trismegistus (Iconographic Documents)

Hermes Trismegistus has been an iconographic subject since the dawn of the Renaissance, even before the rediscovery of the texts of the *Corpus Hermeticum*. He appeared in both Hermetic and alchemical contexts as a figure quite distinct from the alchemical Hermes-Mercury, whose representations fill the numerous treatises on the Great Work illustrated in the seventeenth century.

The Middle Ages did not hesitate to represent this Trismegistus. There is, for example, the beautiful book of illuminations dating from the end of the thirteenth or the beginning of the fourteenth century, at the Meermanno-Westreenianum Museum in The Hague (see Plates 1 and 2). This contains a French version of Saint Augustine's *City of God*, in which the passage that refers to Hermes is illustrated by two miniatures. In the foreground of the first (fol.390) we recognize Jesus and his father; in the background we see the prophet Isaiah, Hermes Trismegistus (who wears a red hat and a blue garment), and Saint Augustine himself. The latter blames Hermes for having described the Egyptian practices that give life to statues with the help of magical formulas and invocations. In so doing, he quotes the relevant passages from the *Asclepius* and says that Hermes has his prophecies on the decline of Egypt from the Devil and not from God. As an example of a "true prophecy" on the decline of Egyptian idolatry, he quotes Isaiah, 19.1: "An oracle concerning Egypt. Behold, the Lord is riding on a swift cloud and comes to Egypt; and the idols of Egypt will tremble at his presence." And in Isaiah 19.10: "Those who are the pillars of the land will be crushed, and all who work for hire will be grieved." The columns from which the statues topple occupy a big place in both pictures; they also illustrate, of course, the famous passage of the "Lamentation" in *Asclepius*. On the second illumination (fol.392), the colors of Hermes Trismegistus's garments are bleaker. He sits weeping as the idols topple from their columns and are collected by devout people, while a mass—the symbol of the true, victorious religion—is celebrated. We are reminded here of Isaiah 19.19: "In that day there will be an altar to the Lord in the midst of the land of Egypt, and a pillar to the Lord at its border."

As far as alchemy is concerned, there are at least three documents from the fifteenth century. We mention first the exquisite illumination in Norton's *Ordinall of Alchymy* (British Library, Add. Ms. 10,302, fol.33 verso). For a colored reproduction, see Stanislas Klossowski, *Alchemy: The Secret Art* (London: Thames and Hudson, 1973), fig. 9. This miniature (Plate 3) shows the bearded heads of four great alchemical Masters, each wearing a hat of a different color and flanked by a scroll with a Latin inscription. The first master, Geber, wears a green hat and says: *"Tere tere tere iterum tere ne tedeat"* (Grind, grind, and ever grind again without ceasing). The second, Arnold of Villanova (blue hat), adds: *"Bibat quantum potest, usque duodenies"* (Let it drink as much as it can, up to twelve times). The third is Rhases (yellow hat): *"Quotiescumque inbibitur totiens dessicatur"* (It must be dried as many times as it was soaked). Lastly Hermes, in a red hat: *"Hoc album aese assate et coquite donec faciat seipsum germinare"* (Roast this white ore and cook it until it grows of itself). These same motifs were redrawn in a different style for Ashmole's collection of English alchemists in 1652 (see Plate 32).

Our second alchemical illustration from the fifteenth century is the watercolor (Plate 4) that accompanies the *Miscellanea di Alchimia* preserved in the Biblioteca Medica Laurenziana in Florence. A double, eight-pointed star accompanies the figure, dressed in Oriental style, who makes a curious gesture with his hands: one finger points upward, those of the other hand downward, as if reminding us of the first verse of the *Emerald Tablet*, "That which is above is like unto that which is below . . ."

The third alchemical illustration from the fifteenth century (Plate 5) occurs in a manuscript of *Aurora Consurgens* with 37 miniatures added to the text (which was not planned with illustration in mind). It is largely a commentary on the *Tabula Chemica* of Senior, i.e., of Ibn Umail: an Arabic text that was very poorly translated into Latin in the twelfth or thirteenth century. There is a bibliography relating to it in the works of Barbara Obrist and Jacques Van Lennep, and in Julius Ruska, "Studien zu Muhammad Ibn Umail" (see note 35 to Chapter 3). The oldest surviving manuscript of *Aurora Consurgens*, albeit an incomplete one, was written between 1420 and 1430, and is in Zurich. The very beautiful complete manuscript of circa 1450, from which our illustration comes, is preserved in Prague. The illumination shown here was published in color by Barbara Obrist, and in black and white by Jacques van Lennep (*Alchimie: Contribution à l'histoire de l'art alchimique*, Crédit Communal de Belgique, 1985). It illustrates the prologue of Senior's book, which tells of the finding, in a sort of temple, of a tablet held in the hands of an old man. This prologue relates the tablet to the Emerald Tablet, and explains the symbolic meaning of the birds. As for the text of the *Tabula Chemica*, it is mainly devoted to the images drawn on this object held by Hermes: purely geometrical figures, without human beings. In this sense, our illustration from the *Aurora Consurgens* is a novelty, since it shows the whole scenario of the discovery, picturing all the elements of the story, even the birds. An almost identical scenario appears in the Arabic text called the *Book of Crates* (end of the eighth or beginning of the ninth century), as well as in other ancient manuscripts that describe the discovery of the emerald "table" or tablet in a crypt, a tomb, a pyramid, or a temple, held in Trismegistus's own hands. Some scenarios present the Tablet as a text (e.g., the *De principalibus rerum causis*); others as a group of figures, as in our Plate 5. This apparently dual tradition of text plus image is in fact a single one; but in the West it is the text that has predominated, to the detriment of the image.

At the base of Plate 5 it says:

Hic jam patet id quod omnibus iis figuris
Ad amico ego dico Senior in Scripturis.

Now is revealed that which, with all these figures,
I, Senior, tell my friend in my writings.

We find this image of Hermes and his tablet surrounded by figures
and birds in several other treatises, of which the first published one
seems to have been the edition of Senior's *Tabula Chemica* circa
1560, under the title *De Chemia* (see Plate 10). This picture was
discussed by Athanasius Kircher in his *Oedipus Aegyptiacus*
(Rome, 1653). The copy of *De Chemia* in the Bibliothèque Nationale
in Paris (Inventaire 33057) is bound with *Ars chemica, quod sit
licita* of 1566. The image is preceded by the following verses:

Quid Soles, Lunae signent, pictaeve tabellae,
Quid venerandi etiam, proflua barba Senis,
Turba quid astantum, volucrum quid turba volantum,
Antra quid, armati quid pedes usque volent.
Miraris? Veterum sunt haec monumenta Sophorum,
Omnia consignans, iste Libellus habet.

Do you wonder what the Sun and Moon mean, and the pictures
of the Tablet; the flowing beard of the venerable old man, the
crowd of people standing there, and the host of birds flying; the
cave, and what the two armed feet signify? These are monu-
ments of the Ancient Sages. That Book has all these things
written on it.

The same artistic motif (see Plate 11) is found in a manuscript
containing several water-colors, done in Nuremberg between 1577
and 1583 (also in Van Lennep's *Alchimie*, p.109). A new printed
adaptation of the motif, less expert than the two preceding, appears
in *Philosophicae Chymicae IV Vetutissima Scripta* (Frankfurt,
1605). Later, the *Theatrum Chemicum* of 1660 (vol. V, p.192) offers

an illustration of the same kind, even less attractive and precise. In Manget's *Bibliotheca Chemica Curiosa* (1702, Vol. II, facing p.216), the drawing has become extremely crude. On this subject, see the commentaries given by J. Ruska in his "Studien" (see above), p.31.

In the context of Hermetism properly so-called, one of the earliest documents is among the 99 drawings executed in Florence in the middle of the fifteenth century or a little after: the *Florentine Picture Chronicle* of Maso Finiguerra or, rather, by his discliple Bacchio Baldini (see Plate 6). It shows scenes and personages of ancient history, both sacred and profane, grouped on 51 leaves (though it appears that one is missing) and done in sepia, grisaille, and brown. Noteworthy figures preceding Hermes Trismegistus include Adam and Eve, Zoroaster, and Ostanes. Discovered in 1840, this manuscript was published with a critical and descriptive text by Sidney Colvin (London: Bernard Quaritch, 1898). Trismegistus holds aloft something resembling a homunculus, perhaps the one of Albertus Magnus, while a kind of nude Hercules, leaning on his club, seems to look on astonished. The legend simply reads: *"Mercurius re di gitto"* (Mercury, King of Egypt). The rocky and chaotic ground reminds one of certain paintings of Leonardo da Vinci.

What is probably the best known work appears not in a book but in Siena Cathedral (see Plate 7). It is one of the images engraved between 1481 and 1498 on the white marble floor-slabs, representing the pagan prophets and the five Sibyls considered as precursors of Christianity; as Ficino says: "Lactantius did not hesitate to number [Trismegistus] among the Sibyls and Prophets." The group in question dates from 1488 and is attributed to Giovanni di Maestro Stephano. Placed in the middle of the floor at the far western end of the building, it immediately seizes the visitor's attention. At the foot it says: *"Hermis Mercurius Trismegistus contemporaneus Moysi"* (Mercury Trismegistus, contemporary of Moses). In the middle he himself appears, with a long forked beard and a pointed hat or miter, handing to another bearded, turbaned man a book on which one can read the words: *"Suscipite o licteras et leges Egiptii"* (Receive your letters and laws, O Egyptians!). His left hand touches a vertical slab supported by sphinxes upon which is carved a passage that summarizes *Asclepius* I, 8. The passage reads:

> *Deus omnium creator*
> *Sec[und]um deum fecit*
> *Visibilem et hunc*
> *Fecit primum et solum*
> *Quo oblectatus est et*
> *Valde amavit proprium*
> *Filium qui appellatur*
> *Sanctum Verbum*

> God, the creator of all, made himself a second visible god, and made him the first and only one. He rejoiced in him, he greatly loved this his own son, who is called the Holy Word.

Some have wondered whether the other personages symbolize savants of West and East (the one on the left is dressed like a monk); or whether Trismegistus is the one in the turban, thus receiving his teachings from Moses. However, it seems more plausible that the central figure is indeed Trismegistus; in fact, as Cicero recalls in his book on the nature of the gods, it was he "who gave laws and letters to the Egyptians." The turbaned man would then be Plato, as Walter Scott suggested in his edition of the *Hermetica* (vol. I, pp.32f.—see Chapter 6, 5B), and the one on the left might well be Marsilio Ficino.

I know of no other representations from this epoch, but there must certainly be some. The gold medal published by Nowotny is perhaps contemporary, on which is written round the edge: *"Hermes Trismegistus philosophus et imperator"* (see Cornelius Agrippa, *De occulta philosophia*, ed. Karl Anton Nowotny, Graz: Akademische Druck- und Verlagsanstalt, 1967: alchemical medal numbered 43).

Should we recognize Trismegistus as one of the three figures of the famous painting by Giorgione—one of the masters of the Venetian School—dating around 1500 and now in the Vienna Staatsgalerie? Here again, we have an old bearded man, holding a manuscript and accompanied by two personages: a turbaned Oriental, and a young, pensive European equipped with square and compasses. The green costume and charming looks of the latter suggest Saint John the Evangelist (compare the illustration by Jean Fouquet in Etienne Chevalier's Book of Hours). The Oriental resembles a picture of an alchemist by Dürer. An X-ray examination of the Giorgione painting has shown that the old man on the right originally wore a diadem with rays, decorated with plumes, such as the ancient Egyptians attributed to the divine scribe, Thoth—here transformed into a mere astrologer. On this painting, see G. F. Hartlaub, "L'ésotérisme de Giorgione (sur un tableau de la Wiener Staatsgalerie)," in *La Tour Saint-Jacques*, no. 15 (May–June 1958), pp.13–18. Mirko Sladek is preparing a thorough study of this painting.

The first Trismegistus of our series who has as attribute an astrolabe or armillary sphere is found at the Ambrosiana Gallery in Milan (Plate 8). Attributed to the Barnabite Brothers, it dates from the second half of the sixteenth century (previously published in *Firenze e la Toscana dei Medici nell Europa del Cinquecento, Catalog of an Exhibition of the Institute and Museum of the History of Science, Florence*: Electra Editrice, Centro Di Edizioni Alinari-Scala, 1980). The sphere is placed, with a compass, beneath a table holding books. It seems that this attribute of our character only appears at this epoch, and often afterwards with the compass, as here. Above the bare head of the figure, a single word "Trismegistus" identifies him. The image is drawn in a circle, on which one reads: "God is an intelligible sphere whose center is everywhere and whose circumference is nowhere"—a formula apparently found for the first time in the twelfth-century *Liber XXIV philosophorum*. (On this book and its fortunes, see Dietrich Mahnke, *Unendliche Sphäre und Allmittelpunkt*, Halle, 1937;

reprinted Stuttgart: F. Fromann, 1966.)

Between 1545 and 1573, the Portuguese artist and humanist Francisco de Holanda completed a superb series of plates entitled *De aetatibus mundi imagines* (facsimile edition with a study by Jorge Segurado, Lisbon, 1983). One of them (fol. 26 verso/LIII/45) represents the entombment of Moses by angels. Two medallions complete this composition, placed one on each side below it. The left-hand one (see Plate 9) shows Hermes Trismegistus in the foreground, flanked by Cadmus and Bacchus in the background. Hermes puts his finger to his lips in the gesture of Harpocrates, like the Hermes-Mercury of the emblem created in that period by Achilles Bocchi (see his *Symbolicae Quaestiones*, 1555, Symbol LXII). The other medallion, below and to the right, represents Lusus, Tantalus, and Perseus. For a bibliography of Francisco d'Holanda, see A. Faivre, "Le *De aetatibus mundi imagines* de Francisco d'Holanda," in *A.R.I.E.S.*, no. 2 (1984), pp.34–37.

Professor Frans A. Janssen has recently drawn my attention to a painting located in a room of the Vatican Library built in 1581 by Francesco Rainaldi for Pope Sixtus V. This room, the Salone Sistino, is located above the present reading room of the Vatican. It contains a series of painted pillars, each representing the "inventor" of a script and of an alphabet. These alphabets are depicted above each corresponding "inventor," and Moses is credited with the invention of Hebrew, Mercurius Thoth with the Egyptian, and so on. The explanatory legends and attributions beneath each of the alphabets are ascribed to Silvio Antoniano and Pietro Galesino, who may have drawn on the studies of Teso Ambrogio and Guillaume Postel. The paintings are ascribed to Luca Horfei. These frescoes belong to the earliest production of the Roman baroque. Soon after the opening of the Library in 1588, three major works were published on the alphabets and their attributions. On the pillar dedicated to Hermes Thoth (see Plates 12A and 12B) we read, inscribed under the character's feet, "Mercurius Thoyt Aegyptiis sacras litteras conscripsit" and above his head an Egyptian alphabet is drawn. He holds the caduceus in his right hand, wears the winged hat, is clad with a white dress, a yellow cloak, a red collar, his belt and breeches are red blue and red. A brooch is affixed on his collar, animals adorn his breeches and a face covered with eyes—therefore identifiable as the head of Argus Panoptes—is painted against his left foot (see Plate 12). On these pillars, and for an extensive bibliography, see *The Type Specimen of the Vatican Press 1628*, facsimile with an introduction and notes by H. D. L. Vervliet (Amsterdam: Menno Hertzberger, 1967), pp.16–21.

Coming now to the seventeenth century, we begin with the great mythological and emblematic work published at Oppenheim: *De divinatione et magicis praestigiis* (see Plate 13). Undated, it comes from the first years of the century and is illustrated by Johann Theodor de Bry, the engraver of numerous plates for Robert Fludd and Michael Maier. The author of the work, Jean-Jacques Boissard, devotes a whole chapter to Hermes Trismegistus, opening with this finely detailed engraving, giving him as attributes an armillary sphere, military trophies, and also—a rare occurrence—a caduceus, to emphasize his kinship with Hermes-Mercury.

An exactly contemporary work (Plate 14), done carelessly as a rapid sketch, scarcely figurative, comes in the work of Giovambatista Birelli: *Opere. Tomo primo. Nel qual si tratta dell'Alchimia, suoi mambri, utili, curiosi, et dilettevoli. Con la vita d'Ermete*, Florence, 1601, p.551. The "life of Hermes" promised in the title occupies no more than a small page.

Still from the beginning of the century, the title page (Plate 15) of Andreas Libavius's *D.O.M.A. Alchymia Andreae Libavii, recognita, emendata, et aucta* (1606), shows Trismegistus accompanied by Hippocrates, Aristotle, and Galen; but none of these is much distinguished from the others by precise attributes. It is one of the first images in which Hermes Trismegistus appears in the company of other personages, assembled in a single tableau with the intent of creating a "monumental" impression (in the etymological sense). This picture is also reproduced as the title page of Libavius's *Syntagmata*, published at Frankfurt in 1611.

The opening page (Plate 16) of the preface of Joachim Tancke's

Promptuarium Alchemiae, vol. I (Leipzig, 1610; facsimile edition with notes and commentaries by Karl R. H. Frick, 2 vols., Graz: Akademische Druck- und Verlagsanstalt, 1976) belongs to the same stylistic current then in formation, failing to give our personage his characteristics and only showing him in schematic form, alongside Geber, Bernard of Trevisan, and Paracelsus. The very elaborate title page (Plate 18) of Oswald Croll's *Basilica Chymica* (Frankfurt, n.d., but dated 1611 in the Duveen catalogue by Kraus) represents Hermes in the company of Morienus, Lull, Geber, and Roger Bacon. The book and its illustration were reissued several times.

This style in question becomes more precise with Michael Maier (see Plate 17), whose work *Symbola aureae mensae duodecim nationum* (Frankfurt, 1617) came from the atelier of Lucas Jennis. A chapter entirely dedicated to Trismegistus opens with an elegant engraving showing the sage holding an armillary sphere in one hand, and with the other pointing to the sun and moon enveloped in circles of fire. One has the impression here that this personage and Hermes-Mercury are one and the same. In the same work, Maier presents twelve sages who speak in turn, after the fashion of the *Turba*, i.e., the "Assemblies" of Hermetic philosophers. Thus on the title page (Plate 19), re-used in the *Musaeum Hermeticum* of 1625 to illustrate another book, "Hermes the Egyptian" is in the place of honor beside Maria the Jewess. One meets him again, face-to-face with Virgil (Plate 20), in a collection of Paracelsus's writings by Johann Huser (Strasburg, 1605; reprint, 1618). The Baroque style of this frontispiece brings out its monumental aspect.

Daniel Stolzius von Stolzenberg, who was practically of the same school as Maier, reproduced our Plate 16 without modification in his *Viridarium Chemicum* (Frankfurt, 1624; Latin and German edition, in which figs. XVIff. are the same as in Maier's *Symbola*). The title page of the book (Plate 21) is flanked by two statues on plinths, Trismegistus and Paracelsus. On these publications, see the postface by Ferdinand Weinhandl to Stolzius's *Chymisches Lustgarten* (Darmstadt: Wissenschaftliche Buchgesellschaft, 1964), and especially the edition of *Viridarium chymicum ou le Jardin chymique* with preface, introduction, translation, and commentaries by Bernard Husson (Paris: Librairie des Médicis, 1975), which is very well documented. In his *Hortulus Hermeticus flosculis philosophorum cupro incisis conformatus . . .* (Frankfurt, 1627, reissued in Manget, vol. II, pp.895ff.), this same Stolzius presents 136 authors and anonymous writers illustrative of the history of alchemy in the form of emblematic medallions (Plate 22). The first of this list is Trismegistus, of whom one can see nothing but a hand emerging from a cloud and holding the armillary sphere. These medallions are actually by Johann Daniel Mylius: they appeared for the first time in 1618, in the third treatise of his *Opus medico-chymicum*, entitled *Basilica philosophica*.

Trismegistus shares the title page of *Hydrolithus Sophicus seu Aquarium Sapientum* (Plate 23) with Galen, Morienus, Lull, Roger Bacon, and Paracelsus. The author of this work is Johann A. Siebmacher (see J. Ferguson, *Bibliotheca Chimica*, vol. II, p.383). The title page in question had already appeared in 1620 in Frankfurt, as a frontispiece to Johann Daniel Mylius's *Operis medico-chymica pars altera*, naturally with a different title in the central panel. Trismegistus is with Hippocrates, Geber, and Aristotle on the title (Plate 24) of the *Pharmacopoea restituta* of Josephus Quercetanus (alias Joseph Duchesne or Du Chesne), Strasburg, 1625. And he faces Hippocrates (Plate 25) on that of the *Via Veritatis Unicae* in the first edition of the *Musaeum Hermeticum* (1625, but absent from the best-known edition, that of 1677. Cf. reprint with introduction by Karl R. H. Frick, Graz: Akademische Druck- und Verlagsanstalt, 1970). Hippocrates accompanies Trismegistus once again, with the allegorical figures of Diligence and Experience (Plate 26), in the *Thesaurus* of Hadrianus à Mynsicht (alias Hanias Madathanus, his real name being Seumenicht), which appeared at Lübeck in 1638 and was several times reissued (e.g., in 1675 at Frankfurt).

Trismegistus's companion is Basil Valentine in the *Traité de l'eau de vie* (1646) of Brouaut, with its beautiful title page (Plate 27):

the only work, so far as I know, in which Trismegistus has as attributes, besides the armillary sphere, both laboratory and musical instruments (a viola da gamba, and seven organ pipes corresponding to the planets). The inscriptions read: *"Psallite Domino in Chordis et organo"* (Sing unto God with strings and organ)— *"Hermes Trismegistus Orientalis Ph[ilosoph]us"* (Hermes Trismegistus, the Oriental Philosopher)—*"Harmonia Sancta, spirituum malignorum fuga seu [Saturn] intemperiei Medicina est"* (Sacred Harmony puts to flight evil spirits and is the Medicine of the intemperate [Saturn]). This engraving was reused in Basile Valentine, *Révélation des mystères des teintures essentielles des sept métaux* (Paris, 1668). A commentary on it appears in Eugène Canseliet, *Deux Logis alchimiques* (Paris: Pauvert, 1979), pp.237–241.

On the *Pharmacopoeia Augustana* of 1646, Trismegistus carries the text of the *Emerald Tablet* written on a scroll and faces Hippocrates (Plate 28). It is Hippocrates, Galen, and Aristotle who accompany Hermes (Plate 29) in the *Recueil des plus curieux et rares secrets* (1648), a collection of various works by Joseph Duchesne, alias Quercetanus. This elegant title page was engraved by Michel Van Lochen in 1641. The frontispiece of *Ars Medica* (Plate 30), another posthumous edition of Quercetanus's works, shows Hermes Trismegistus opposite Galen, together with several drawings inside squares that illustrate the medical art.

This style of presentation, with multiple emblematic personages or scenes, is quite common in this period: among the best known examples is the frontispiece of Robert Burton's *Anatomy of Melancholy* (Oxford, 1628). A simplified version of the pattern (Plate 31) appears in the treatise of Rhumelius, *Medicina Spagyrica* (Frankfurt, 1648), with Hermes Trismegistus standing opposite Arnold of Villanova. Beneath Hermes is a sick room; beneath Arnold, an apothecary's shop. At bottom center is a kind of athanor; at top center, a dove descends from heaven to earth, where two serpents arise.

In 1652 a modernized version of the fifteenth-century Norton's

Ordinall was published in the *Theatrum Chemicum Britannicum* of Elias Ashmole (Plate 32). This was the work of Robert Vaughan, engraver of similar plates in the works of Henry and Thomas Vaughan; on him, see M. Corbett and M. Morton, eds., *Engraving in England in the 16th and 17th Centuries,* Part 3: "The Reign of Charles I" (Cambridge University Press, 1964); and the Index of Alan Rudrum, *The Works of Thomas Vaughan* (Oxford University Press, 1984).

Another reworking of earlier materials (Plate 33) shows Trismegistus in company with Paracelsus, with a central motif inspired by Robert Fludd. This was first brought to notice and reproduced in Allen G. Debus, *The Chemical Philosophy* (New York: Science History Publications, 1977), vol. II, p.515, who pointed out that the portraits of Hermes and Paracelsus derive from those on the title page of Oswald Croll's *Basilica Chymica* (see our Plate 18), while the central image is a copy of a well-known engraving by Johann Theodor de Bry in the first part of Robert Fludd's *Utriusque cosmi historia* (Oppenheim, 1617). Hermes says: *"Quod est superius, est sicut quod est inferius"* (What is above is like that which is below—the opening words of the *Emerald Tablet*); Paracelsus: *"Separate et ad maturitatem perducite"* (Separate and lead it on to ripeness). This montage is the work of Tobias Schütze (*Harmonia macrocosmi cum microcosmo,* Frankfurt, 1654.) After the middle of the century there do not seem to have been many new works.

It would be fruitful to explore systematically the nonalchemical illustrations of the late Renaissance period, particularly the emblem collections. For instance, George Wither's *A Collection of Emblemes, Ancient and Modern* (1635) reproduces emblematic works already published by Gabriel Rollhagen in *Nucleus emblematum selectissimorum* (Utrecht, circa 1611–1613): in the "Choice of Hercules" (Plate 34), an odd allegory, the personage on the left is certainly not Mercury, but the beard, caduceus, and book are the attributes of Trismegistus.

Later on, "trismegistic" illustrations become very scarce, and as

we know, the eighteenth century is far less rich in esoteric illustrated documents than the seventeenth. Thus the only eighteenth-
century document of which I am aware (though others must exist)
is not an illustration on paper, but a painting on wood panel, 63 x
142 cms. (see Plate 35). Anonymous, and probably done around
1740, it comes from the Pharmacy of the Court of Innsbruck
(Innsbrucker Hofapotheke). There are three panels which seem to
have made up a kind of triptych, serving as the door to an apothecary's
cupboard. Just after World War II it was still in Innsbruck in the
house called "Zum Goldenen Dach," but was purchased shortly
after by the Schweizerisches Pharmazie-historisches Museum in
Basel, where this triptych is currently exhibited (historical information kindly furnished by Dr. Michael Kessler, Curator of the
Museum, during my visit in April 1991 and in a letter of 10 June
1991).

Hermes Trismegistus here carries his traditional attribute, the
armillary sphere, in his right hand, and in the left a scroll on which
is written the first verse of the *Emerald Tablet*. The predominant
colors are red and blue: red for his robe (the large cape is white) and
blue for his cloak, belt, and hat. The two other panels are by the
same hand: one represents Hippocrates, the other Aesculapius.
Originally, Trismegistus probably stood between the two physicians, but nowadays the three panels are displayed separately,
though in the same room.

One of the Egyptianizing masonic rituals of the late eighteenth
century (or around 1800) is called "Die Magier von Memphis" (The
Magi of Memphis). It has two side-degrees centered around the
figure of Hermes Trismegistus. These degrees are called "Sublime
Philosopher of Hermes" and "Sublime Magus of Memphis." In the
setting of the lodge, a drawing represents Hermes Trismegistus
rising from a grave. He is flanked by two branches of laurel and a
Delta hovers above his head. This picture corresponds to the
initiation practice in the ritual: after the candidate has entered the
lodge, a Brother hidden in a coffin opens the lid from within and
rises. This Brother impersonates Hermes Trismegistus and ex-

plains that he, Hermes Trismegistus, has emerged from the night of the tomb in order to deliver the candidate from error and confusion. He declares that he has a knowledge of "the most profound mysteries of Nature" and he claims: "This science, I, Hermes, taught the priests and kings of Egypt. They taught each other and achieved the most surprising things, simply by imitating the process of Nature. These secrets were the objects of the Royal Art." After dwelling on the history of the transmission of that knowledge, he concludes by saying: "Remember me. My true name is Mercurius for the Egyptians, Thoth for the Phoenicians, Hermes Trismegistus for the Greeks, and all over the earth I am Hiram, whose wonderful story has amazed you."

It is the only masonic ritual I know that identifies Hermes Trismegistus with Hiram, that is with the mythical architect of King Solomon's Temple. In most masonic rituals, Hiram is murdered by two of his companions and then rises from the grave, a scenario enacted by the candidate to the Master degree. The original manuscript of the ritual "The Magus of Memphis" was written in French and preserved at the Freimaurer Museum Library of Bayreuth. It was translated into German in 1928 (by Otto Schaaf, pp.207–245 in *Das Freimaurer-Museum: Archiv für freimaurerische Ritualkunde und Geschichtsforschung*, vol. IV, Zeulenroda/Leipzig: B. Sporn, 1928, under the title "Zwei Hochgrad-Rituale des 18. Jahrhunderts"). This manuscript is lost without having been published in its original form in French, and was already lost in 1978 (see Karl R. H. Frick, *Licht und Finsternis*, vol. II, Graz: Akad. Druck- und Verlagsanstalt, 1978, pp.149–157). Fortunately, Otto Schaaf not only published the translation he made into German, but also provided beautiful reproductions of the original nine manuscript illustrations (copies made by Carl Kämpe, see O. Schaaf, *op. cit.*, p.209), one of which is reproduced here (Plate 36). It is the only one featuring Hermes Trismegistus.

Beside other documents of this kind on paper or canvas of which I am not yet aware, there is a drawing (Plate 37) made at the start of the nineteenth century by the theosopher, kabbalist, and alchemist Johann Friedrich von Meyer (on whom see Jacques Fabry, *Le théosophe allemand Johann Friedrich von Meyer [1772–1849]*, Berne: Peter Lang, 1989). Meyer decorated the title page of one of his manuscript works devoted to these fields of esotericism and called *Cabala Magica et theosophica* with a bearded head that is none other than our Trismegistus.

Finally we note two examples from our own century. First, Plate 38 reproduces Augustus Knapp's painting of Hermes Trismegistus; he is dressed from head to toe in Egyptian fashion, holding a caduceus in one hand and a book in the other, while pinning to the ground with one foot a live, fire-breathing dragon This is one of the most curious figures in the esoteric picture gallery of Manly P. Hall's *The Secret Teachings of All Ages: An Encyclopedic Outline of Masonic, Hermetic, Qabbalistic, and Rosicrucian Symbolical Philosophy* (Los Angeles: Philosophical Research Society, 1928 and subsequent issues).

Second (Plate 39), in the most extensive encyclopedia of Tarot, cogently compiled, presented, and commented upon by its author, Stuart R. Kaplan, we find the "Neti Neti Tibetan Tarot." This deck is dated 1952 and was worked out by the "Christian Community." Card 19 shows a *herma*, i.e. a post surmounted with the head of Hermes, in front of a fountain basin. In ancient Greece the so-called *hermae* were placed as crossroads and entrance ways. Here, the head of the *herma* is reminiscent of a priest or sage, and a caption beneath the image reads "Trismegistos" in Greek letters. So this picture has a twofold connotation, that of Mercury and that of Hermes Trismegistus. The deck claims to draw on various traditions, not only Egyptian and Greek, but also Chinese, Christian, and—as the title of the deck already warns us—Tibetan.

This collection of images does not pretend to be at all exhaustive. All suggestions for references and new lines of investigation sent to the author in care of Phanes Press will be gratefully acknowledged.

Plates 1 and 2. Two illuminations from a French mansucript entitled *Augustinus: Cité de Dieu* (fols. 390, 392). End of 13th or beginning of 14th century. The Hague, Museum Meermanno-Westreenianum. Professor Frans A. Janssen kindly called my attention to this document. It is reproduced by courtesy of the Museum.

Plate 3. Norton's *Ordinall of Alchymy*, 15th century. British Library, Add. Ms. 10,302, fol. 32'. By permission of the British Library.

Plate 4. "Pater Hermes philosophorum." Watercolor from *Miscellanea di Alchimia*, 15th century. Florence, Biblioteca Medicea Laurenziana. Kindly communicated to me by Dr. Mirko Sladek.

Plate 5. Illustration from a manuscript of *Aurora Consurgens* (University Library in Prague, Ms. VI fd 26), second quarter of the 15th century. See also Plates 10 and 11.

Plate 6. Maso Finiguerra or Bacchio Baldini, *A Florentine Picture Chronicle, being a series of ninety-nine drawings representing scenes and personages of ancient history, sacred and profane.* London: Bernard Quaritch, 1898. Middle of the 15th century.

Plate 7. Inlaid floor panel from Siena Cathedral, 1488, by Giovanni di Maestro Stephano.

Plate 8. From a manuscript astrolabe, attributed to the Barnabite Fathers, second half of the 16th century. Milan, Ambrosiana.

Plate 9. Francisco de Holanda, *De aetatibus mundi imagines*, between 1545 and 1573 (National Library of Madrid, B Artes 14–26). Medallion placed beneath the "Death of Moses," fol. 26'/LII/45.

Plate 10. *De chemia senioris antiquissimi philosophi, libellus, ut brevis, ita artem discentibus, et exercentibus, utilissimus et vere aureus, nunc primum in lucem aeditus. Ab artis fideli filio,* dixit Senior Zadith Filius Hamuel. No place, no date; circa 1560. See also Plates 5 and 11.

Plate 11. Extract from an alchemical manuscript containing various watercolors, Nuremberg (Germanisches Nationalmuseum, Ms. 16752), between 1577 and 1583. See also Plates 5 and 10.

Plate 12A and 12B. Painting on a column of the Salone Sistine (Vatican Library). The series of column-paintings in that room is attributed to Luca Horfei (1587) and represents the "inventors" of scripts and alphabets. Here, Mercurius Thoth is the inventor of the Egyptian ("Mercurius Thoyt Aegyptiis sacras litteras conscripsit"). Above Hermes, an Egyptian alphabet. Professor Frans A. Janssen kindly called my attention to this document.

Plate 13. Jean-Jacques Boissard, *De divinatione et magicis praestigiis*, Oppenheim, no date (circa 1616). Engraving by Johann Theodor de Bry, the illustrator of Robert Fludd and Michael Maier.

Plate 14. Giovambatista Birelli, *Opere*, vol. I: *Nel qual si tratta dell'Alchimia . . . Con la vita d'Ermete*, Florence, 1601, p.551. By permission of the British Library.

Plate 15. Andreas Libavius. *D.O.M.A. Alchymia Andreae Libavii, recognita, emendata, et aucta* (1606). Reproduced as the title page of Libavius's *Syntagma Selectorum . . .* (Frankfurt, 1611) and *Syntagmatis Arcanorum Chymicorum* (Frankfurt, 1613).

Plate 16. Joachim Tancke, *Promptuarium Alchemiae*, vol. I, Leipzig, 1610. From the Author's Preface.

Plate 17. Michael Maier, *Symbola aureae mensae duodecim nationum*, Frankfurt, 1617, p.5.

Plate 18. Oswald Croll, *Basilica Chymica*, Frankfurt, no date (1629, first ed. 1608). The same design was used in the Latin edition, 1611. By permission of Thames & Hudson, Ltd.

Plate 19. *Gloria Mundi. Alias, Paradysi Tabula.* In *Musaeum Hermeticum*, Frankfurt,1624. By permission of the Bibliotheca Philosophica Hermetica, Amsterdam. First published in Michael Maier's *Symbola* (cf. *supra*, Plate 17).

Plate 20. Paracelsus, *Chirurgische Bücher und Schrifften*, edited by Johann Huser, Strasburg, 1605; reprint, 1618. By permission of the British Library.

Plate 21. Daniel Stolzius von Stolzenberg, *Chymisches Lustgärtlein*, Frankfurt, 1624.

Plate 22. Daniel Stolzius von Stolzenberg, *Hortulus Hermeticus Flosculis Philosophorum Cupro Incisis Conformatus . . .*, from Manget's *Bibliotheca Chemica Curiosa*, Geneva, 1702, vol. II, p.896. These medallions appeared first in 1618, in the third treatise of Johann Daniel Mylius's *Opus medico-chymicum*. By permission of Thames & Hudson, Ltd.

Plate 23. Anonymous [=Johann Ambrosius Siebmacher], *Hydrolithus Sophicus seu Aquarium Sapientum,* in *Musaeum Hermeticum,* Frankfurt, 1625. By permission of the Bibliotheca Philosophica Hermetica, Amsterdam.

Plate 24. Josephus Quercetanus (alias Joseph Du Chesne), *Pharmacopoea restituta*, Strasburg, 1625.

Plate 25. Anonymous, *Via Veritatis Unicae. Hoc est, elegans, perutile et praetans opusculum, viam Veritatis aperiens.* Probably written at the turn of the 15th to 16th century. This illustration accompanies the work in the collection *Musaeum Hermeticum*, Frankfurt, 1625. By permission of Thames & Hudson, Ltd.

Plate 26. Hadrianus à Mynsicht, *Thesaurus et [...] Armamentarium Medico-Chymicum. Cui in fine adjunctum est Testamentum Hadrianeum de Aureo Philosophorum Lapide.* Lübeck, 1638 (first ed., Hamburg, 1631).

Plate 27. Jean Brouaut, *Traité de l'eau de vie*, Paris, 1646. By permission of the Bibliotheca Philosophica Hermetica, Amsterdam.

Plate 28. *Pharmacopoeia Augustana*, Augsburg, 1646. Illustration by Mattheus Gundelach and Wolfgang Kilian. By permission of the British Library.

Plate 29. Josephus Quercetanus (alias Joseph Du Chesne), *Recueil des plus curieux et rares secrets . . .*, Paris, 1648. Title page by Michael van Lochem, 1641, of a posthumous collection of Du Chesne's writings.

Plate 30. Josephus Quercetanus (alias Joseph Du Chesne), *Quercetanus Redivivus, hoc est Ars Medica Hermetica*, Frankfurt, 1648. By permission of the British Library.

Plate 31. Johann Pharamund Rhumelius, *Medicina Spagyrica oder Spagyrische Artzneukynst*, Frankfurt, 1648. By permission of the British Library.

Plate 32. Elias Ashmole, *Theatrum Chemicum Britannicum*, London, 1652, p.44. A redrawing of Plate 1 for Ashmole's edition of Norton's *Ordinall*. By permission of the British Library.

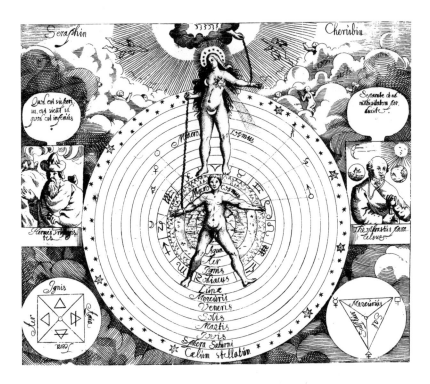

Plate 33. Tobias Schütze, *Harmonia macrocosmi cum microcosmo,* Frankfurt, 1654. Based on Croll (see Plate 17) and on illustrations of the *Utriusque cosmi historia* (1617) of Robert Fludd.

Plate 34. George Wither, *A Collection of Emblemes, Ancient and Modern*, London, 1635, Book I, Emblem 22. By permission of the British Library.

Plate 35. Anonymous painting, circa 1740, formerly in the Court Pharmacy of Innsbruck, now in the Schweizerisches Pharmazie-historisches Museum, Basel. By permission of the Museum.

Plate 36. Hermes Trismegistus rising from the grave in order to teach the candidate an initiation. Masonic ritual of "The Magus of Memphis," end of the eighteenth century or around 1800. From "Zwei Hochgrad-Rituale des 18. Jahrhunderts," pp.207–245 in *Das Freimaurer-Museum: Archiv für freimaurerische Ritualkunde und Geschichtsforschung*, vol. IV, Zeulenroda/Leipzig: B. Sporn, 1928 (see p.212). By permission of the Oscar Schlag Library, Zurich.

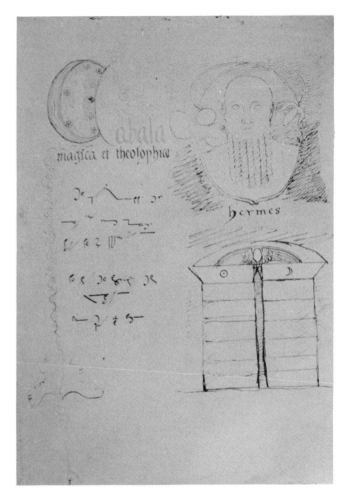

Plate 37. Johann Friedrich von Meyer, extract from unpublished manuscript *Cabala magica et theosophica*, circa 1805 (Erlangen, Theologische Fakultät, Institut für Historische Theologie). Document kindly furnished by Jacques Fabry.

Plate 38. Augustus Knapp, color painting of Hermes Trismegistus, from Manly P. Hall, *The Secret Teachings of All Ages* (Los Angeles: Philosophical Research Society, 1928). By permission of the Philosophical Research Society in Los Angeles.

Plate 39. Card 19, "Trismegistos," from the Tarot deck "Neti Neti Tibetan Tarot" (Christian Community, 1952). From Stuart R. Kaplan, *The Encyclopedia of the Tarot*, volume III (Stamford, CT: U.S. Games Systems, 1990), p.392. By permission of U.S. Games Systems, Inc.

CHAPTER SIX

The Inheritance of Alexandrian Hermetism: Historical and Bibliographical Landmarks

The majority of the Greek texts known as the Hermetica were written in Alexandria or the Nile Delta at the beginning of the Christian Era. Some of them (second to third centuries), like those collected later under the title of *Corpus Hermeticum*, are attributed to the legendary Hermes Trismegistus. This corpus was practically lost during the whole Medieval period, with the exception of the book *Asclepius*, preserved in Latin translation and subsequently reunited with the other texts. Nevertheless, the tradition started by these Hermetica persisted up to the Renaissance, when it was assured of a lasting success by the rediscovery, in 1460, of the *Corpus Hermeticum*. Until 1614 the latter was believed, along with its mythical author Hermes Trismegistus, to be at least as ancient as Moses.

The following data make no pretention other than as landmarks. They concern the reception of Alexandrian Hermetism both as such, and as considered in its long-term effects, particularly in the esoteric field.

1. The Middle Ages

1A. Some references to Hermes Trismegistus and to the *Asclepius* in the early Church Fathers:

Clement of Alexandria (third century), *Stromata* VI, 4, 35–38.

Lactantius (fourth century), *Divinae Institutiones* I, 6; IV, 6; II. VIII, 18.

Augustine (fifth century), *De civitate dei* 410–426: VIII, 13–26, XVIII, 29.

For complete listing of the "Testimonia," see A. S. Ferguson and W. Scott, cited below (5B), vol. 4.

1B. Among the Medieval authors mentioning Hermes Trismegistus or citing the *Asclepius*:

Michael Psellus, Byzantine Platonist of the eleventh century, uses the Hermetic and Orphic texts to explain the Scriptures.

Theodoric of Chartres; Albertus Magnus; Bernard Silvestris; Alain of Lille; William of Auvergne; Thomas Bradwardine; Roger Bacon; Bernard of Treviso; Hugh of Saint Victor. From the ninth century onwards, many Arabic writings draw their inspiration from Greek sources, which then return to the West through Latin translations.

1C. Some Medieval texts influenced by the spirit of Alexandrian Hermetism:

Between Late Antiquity and the Renaissance there appeared a great number of texts in Latin, in the wake of Alexandrian Hermeticism and often attributed to the mythical Hermes Trismegistus. The *Picatrix* (tenth century), translated from the Arabic, and many other texts were followed in the twelfth century by other metaphysical and cosmological writings like the *De sex rerum principiis* and the *Liber viginti quatuor philosophorum*. Writings like the *Centiloquium*, the *Kyranides*, the *Liber Lunae* and the *Tabula Smaragdina* were widely disseminated and penetrated Latin culture. The collection *Hermes Latinus* (Corpus Christianorum, Continuatio Mediaevalis, Brepols N.V. in Belgium), currently in preparation under the direction of Paolo Lucentini, will present most of these Latin texts.

2. Rediscovery at the Renaissance

2A. The point of departure:

In 1460, Leonardo da Pistoia, a monk, brought to Florence a Greek manuscript of the *Corpus Hermeticum*, almost complete (fifteen treatises), which he had discovered in Macedonia. These were thus "new" texts, because the only item of this collection known was the *Asclepius* in Latin. At the end of 1462, Cosimo de' Medici had it translated into Latin by Marsilio Ficino, thinking this a more urgent job than that of the works of Plato. Until the end of the sixteenth century there were no fewer than sixteen editions, not counting partial ones. Ficino's translation went through twenty-five editions between 1471 and 1641. The commentaries accompanying these editions are often of considerable interest.

Pico della Mirandola contributed to the success of the *Corpus Hermeticum* by forging an esoteric alliance between Kabbalism and Hermetism. Out of this was born a Hermetic art, e.g., in Botticelli's *Primavera* (1478); Siena Cathedral pavement (1488); Borgia Apartments in the Vatican, decorated by Pinturicchio, etc.

2B. Remarks on English Puritanism, and the situation in Germany:

Essentially gnostic and irenic, the religious Hermetism of post-Medieval times flourished in places where tolerance prevailed—at the same time as favoring the latter. During the sixteenth century it was not welcomed in England either by Puritanism or by Hispano-Catholic policy.

As is well known, the Lutheranism of the Germanic countries delayed the reception of Humanism. This is why the *Corpus Hermeticum*, which arose out of Humanist culture, penetrated less into Germany than elsewhere. But in the Germanic countries, other esoteric currents (theosophy of Weigel and Boehme, Paracelsism, Rosicrucianism) compensated in the sixteenth and seventeenth centuries for this absence. Germanic theosophy scarcely ever alludes to Hermes Trismegistus.

2C. Some editions and commentaries on the *Corpus Hermeticum*:

In 1463, Ficino's translation of *Corpus Hermeticum* I–XIV was finished. It was printed in 1471 at Treviso: *Mercurii Trismegisti Pimander, seu liber de potestate et sapientia Dei.**

William Caxton, *The dictes or sayensis of the philosophers*, 1477 (numerous subsequent editions, notably by William Baldwin and Thomas Palfreyman in the sixteenth century).

John Doget, *Examinatorium in Phaedonem Platonis*, end of the fifteenth century.

Lefèvre d'Etaples, *Pimander* (*Corpus Hermeticum* I–XVI) (Paris, 1494; and 1505 with the *Crater Hermetis* of Ludovico Lazzarelli and *Asclepius*). Lazarelli, who translated treatise XVI (which Ficino had not known), was probably also the author of *Epistola Enoch*, a work in the same tradition. The commentaries on the *Pimander* were by Lefèvre, not Ficino.

Giovanni Nesi, *Oraculum de novo saeculo* (Florence, 1497).

Aureum planeque opusculum Mercurii Trismegisti, de potestate ac sapientia dei, presented by Johann Scheffler (Augsburg, 1503).

Il Pimandro di Mercurio Trismegisto (Florence, 1548; new edition, 1549), translated into Italian by Tommaso Benci (translation dating from 1463).

Mercure Trismégiste Hermès Très ancien Théologien et excellent Philosophe: de la puissance et sapience de Dieu [. . .]. Avec un dialogue de Loys Lazarel intitulé le Bassin d'Hermès (Paris, 1549). This is the edition in French by Gabriel du Préau of the *Pimander*, together with the *Crater Hermetis* of Lazarelli. New edition in 1557.

Partial edition by Trincavelli of the *Fragments of Stobaeus* (Venice, 1553/1556), completed in 1575 by Canter.

---

* The first treatise of the *Corpus Hermeticum* is entitled *Pimander*, or *Poimandres*, which is why this title replaces "*Corpus Hermeticum*" in many editions.

First edition of the Greek text of the *Corpus Hermeticum* by Turnebus (Paris, 1554), with Vergerius's preface, the Latin translation of Ficino and the commentaries of Lefèvre.

New Greco-Latin edition of the *Pimander* (Bordeaux, 1574), by Bishop Foix de Candale, followed Bordeaux, 1579 by its French edition, with extensive French commentary *(Le Pimandre de Mercure Trismégiste, de la philosophie chrestienne, cognoissance du Verbe divin)*; reissued Paris, 1587.

Basel edition of Ficino's *Opera* (1576), with numerous passages concerning Hermetism.

Enormous edition, with commentary, by the Italian Franciscan Hannibal Rossel, *Pymander Mercurii Trismegisti*, 6 vols. (Krakow, 1585/1590; reissued Cologne, 1 vol., 1630).

Circa 1580, Dutch translation of the XVI Books (complete and unpublished, Ms. in Antwerp), probably inspired by that of Foix de Candale.

Nova de universis philosophia by Francesco Patrizi (Ferrara, 1591; reissued Venice, 1593), which contains the *Corpus Hermeticum* after the text of Turnebus and Foix de Candale, together with a new Latin translation and a vigorous defence of Hermetism.

Sir Philip Sidney: publication in 1587 of his English translation of the book by Du Plessis-Mornay (see next section).

2D. Some authors whose work is more or less marked by this Hermetism:

Symphorien Champier, *Liber de quadruplici vita. Theologia Asclepii Hermetis Trismegisti discipuli cum commentariis eiusdem* (Lyon, 1507).

Thomas More, *Life of Picus* (1510) and *Utopia* (1516).

Johann Trithemius, *De septem secundeis* (Nuremberg, 1522).

Francesco Giorgi of Venice, *De harmonia mundi* (Venice, 1525; French translation by Guy Lefèvre de la Boderie, Paris, 1579) and *Problemata* (Paris, 1536).

Heinrich Cornelius Agrippa, *De occulta philosophia* (Cologne,

1533), and several treatises (1515, 1516).

Agostino Steuco, *De perenni philosophia* (Lyon, 1540 and 1590). This Italian Augustinian expounds in his book the idea of a "perennial philosophy," and of a tradition of which Hermes Trismegistus is one of the representatives.

Giulio Camillo Delminio, *L'Idea del theatro* (Florence and Venice, 1550), and several other writings between 1530 and 1544.

John Dee, *Propaedeumata Aphoristica* (1558, reissued 1568), and *Monas Hieroglyphica* (Antwerp, 1565).

Guy Lefèvre de la Boderie, *La Galliade* (Paris, 1578).

Pontus de Tyard, *Les discours philosophiques* (Paris, 1578).

Philippe Du Plessis-Mornay, *De la vérité de la religion chrestienne* (Antwerp, 1582).

Alexander Dicson, *De umbra rationis* (London, 1584).

Edmund Spenser, *The Fairie Queen* (London, 1590/1596).

Giordano Bruno, Valentin Weigel, Michael Servetius, Jacques Gohory, Du Bartas, Richard Hooker.

3. Casaubon's "Revelation" and the Seventeenth Century

3A. Isaac Casaubon:

This Genevan Protestant proved in 1614 (*De rebus sacris ecclesiasticis exercitationes XVI* published in London) that the texts of the *Corpus Hermeticum* are no earlier than the first centuries of the Christian Era. Some Hermetists deliberately ignored this discovery, others remained unaware of it; but little by little, Alexandrian Hermetism found fewer admirers and commentators, since it was now known to be far less ancient than had been believed. For the situation in Germany, see above, section 2B.

It still became the object of some presentations, adaptations, and translations, including:

Extracts from the *Corpus Hermeticum* in German: "Verba Hermetis in Pimandro," in *Occulta Philosophia*, vol. II (Frankfurt, 1613).

First edition of a Dutch translation, in the work *Wonder-Vondt van de eeuwighe bewegingh die den Alckmaersche Philosoph Cornelis Drebbel . . .* (Alkmaar, 1607), the XVI Books. (This translation owes nothing to the Ms. one of 1580, mentioned above.)
Reissue of the *Pimander* by Rossel (1585; see Section 2.C) (Cologne, 1630).
Dutch translation of the XVI Books of the *Corpus Hermeticum* (Amsterdam, 1643, reissued 1652) by Abraham Willemsz. Van Beyerland (the translator of Jacob Boehme): *Sesthien Boecken met groote naarstigheyt van den Voor-trefflicken ouden Philosoph, Hermes Trismegistus*, translated from the Latin text of Francesco Patrizi.

Hermes Mercurius Trismegistus, his Divine Pymander, in XVII books, English translation presented by John Everard (London, 1650). Reissued in 1657, with the *Asclepius* and commentaries by Lefèvre d'Etaples.

3B. Some authors whose work is more or less marked by this Hermetism:

Mutius Pansa, *De Osculo seu consensu ethnicae et christianae philosophiae* (Marburg, 1605).

Jean-Pierre Camus, *Diversités* (Paris, 1609, 1615).

Sir Walter Raleigh, *History of the World* (London, 1609).

Philippe Cluver, *Germaniae antique libri tres* (Lyon, 1616), vol. I.

Henricus Nollius, *Theoria philosophiae hermeticae* (Copenhagen, 1617).

Joseph Stellatus (pseudonym for Christoph Hirsch), *Pegasus Firmamenti. Sive introductio brevis in Veterum Sapientiam* (n.p., 1618).

Robert Fludd, *Utriusque cosmi historia* (Oppenheim, 1617–1621).

Johannes Kepler, *Harmonices mundi libri V* (Linz, 1619).

Robert Burton, *The Anatomy of Melancholy* (Oxford, 1621).

Livius Galante, *Christianae Theologiae cum platonica*

comparatio (Bologna, 1627).

John Milton, *Il Penseroso* (London, 1645).

Hermann Conring, *De Hermetica Aegyptiorum vetere et paracelsicorum nova medicina* (Helmstedt, 1648 and 1669): speaks much of Hermetism, but generally as an opponent, and against Borrichius, cited below.

Jean d'Espagnet, *La Philosophie naturelle rétablie en sa pureté, avec le Traité de l'Ouvrage secret d'Hermès* (Paris, 1651).

Athanasius Kircher, *Prodromus coptus* (Rome, 1636); *Oedipus Aegyptiacus* (Rome, 1652–1654).

Johann Heinrich Ursinus, *De Zoroastre Bactriano, Hermete Trismegisto . . .* (Nuremberg, 1661).

Olaus Borrichius, *Hermetis Aegyptiorum et chemicorum sapientia* (Copenhagen, 1674). *De ortu et progressio chemiae* (Copenhagen, 1668).

Ralph Cudworth, *The True Intellectual System of the Universe* (London, 1678). Also several writings of Henry More.

W. Chr. Kriegsmann, *Conjectaneorum de Germanicae gentis origine, de conditore, Hermete Trismegisto* (Tübingen, 1684).

Johann Ludovicus Hannemann, *Ovum hermetico-paracelsico-trismegistum* (Frankfurt, 1694).

4. In the Eighteenth and Nineteenth Centuries

4A. General remarks:

After the end of the seventeenth century, "Trismegistian" Hermetism was of less interest as such than as an opportunity to evoke a very general current with which it was more or less confused. This current mixed up Egyptomania, Orphism, Pythagoreanism, Kabbalah, and Paracelsism. "Hermeticism" is used increasingly as a synonym for "alchemy," even for "Rosicrucianism." (See the footnote on page 39, concerning the use of the terms "Hermetism" and "Hermeticism.") Representative of this tendency to put together various esoteric traditions under the heading "Hermetic" is the book by Daniel Colberg, *Das Platonisch-*

Hermetische Christentum (Frankfurt, 1690–91; new edition, 1710), whose title and contents betray a mish-mash of theosophy, alchemy, Kabbalah, and Hermetism.

Some works in eighteenth-century Germany still evidence interest in the *Corpus Hermeticum*. In the nineteenth century it was above all the Anglo-Saxon countries that took up the thread, but not before the second half of the century. In France, we should mention the work of Louis Ménard: *Hermès Trismégiste. Traduction complète, précédée d'une étude sur l'origine des libres hermétiques* (Paris, 1866, several times reissued).

Hermetism still has an underground influence in the nineteenth century, more or less diffuse, whose importance is only beginning to be recognized. On its influence on Anglo-Saxon literature, see especially the important study of E. L. Tuveson, cited below, section 6A. Naturally all its repercussions cannot be mentioned in the limited compass of this survey, which is restricted to some of the most obvious manifestations of "explicit" Hermetism.

4B. German works:

The first German translation of the *Pimander* appeared in Hamburg, 1706, with a thorough hermetizing commentary by "Alethophilus" (probably W. von Metternich), under the title *Erkänntnüsz der Natur and des sich darin offenbahrenden Grossen Gottes* (reissued 1786, and Stuttgart, 1855).

Hermes Trismegistus and the *Corpus Hermeticum* are present in a number of literary and/or philosophical works in Germany (like J. G. Herder's *Aelteste Urkunde des Menschengeschlechts*, 1774/1775 and his *Adrastea*, 1802), and in some Masonic rituals like the interesting "Magi of Memphis," which is perhaps a French ritual.

Two important works contributed to making Alexandrian thought better known, presenting it in a more general historical context:

(a) *Bibliotheca Graeca*, by Johann Albert Fabricius (14 vols., Hamburg, 1705/1728); see particularly Lib. I, cap. vii–xii, vol. I, 1708. The whole series was reissued with additions and corrections in Hamburg (see vol. I, 1790).

(b) *Historia critica Philosophiae*, by J. Brucker, whose first and fourth volumes (Leipzig, 1743) are entirely given to Hermetism and theosophy in the broad sense.

Johann Mosheim published at Jena, 1733, a Latin translation of works by Ralph Cudworth (*Systema intellectuale hujus universi*), with hermetizing commentaries.

Dieterich Tiedemann, *Hermes Trismegisti Poemander* (Berlin, 1781).

Gustav Parthey, *Hermes Trismegisti Poemander* (Berlin, 1854); also his *Jamblichi "De Mysteriis"* (Berlin, 1857).

B. J. Hilgers, *De Hermetis Trismegisti Poimandro Commentatio* (Bonn, 1855).

R. Pietschmann, *Hermes Trismegistos, nach ægyptischen, griechischen und orientalischen Ueberlieferungen dargestellt* (Leipzig, 1875).

New edition of Aletophilos's German translation of 1706, with a long introduction on Hermes Trismegistus and on the *Emerald Tablet*, by J. Scheible: *Hermetis Trismegisti Einleitung ins höchste Wissen* (Stutgart, 1855), in the esoteric series "Kleiner Wunderschauplatz der geheimen Wissenschaften, Mysterien, Theosophie . . . ," vol. I.

4C. Reawakening in England and the United States

"An Egyptian Testimony to the actual Observation of the Spiritual World. The Poemander of Hermes Trismegistus," in *The Supernatural Magazine* (Dublin), no. 3 (August 1809), pp.75–83. Everard's translation of the *Pimander* and the *Key*.

Publication of the *Pimander* in *The Dial* (a New England journal of spiritual leanings), vol. IV (1844).

The Divine Pymander of Hermes Mercurius Trismegistus (Whittlesey: J. Green, n.d., but dated ?1850 by the British Library). Contains the *88 Sentences* and *Pimander*, with "To the Reader" by J. F.

Hermes Mercurius Trismegistus; his Divine Pymander, ed. Paschal Beverly Randolph, with prefatory material by Flora S. Russel

(Boston, Mass.: "Rosicrucian Publishing Co.," 1871, reissued 1889).

From 1880 onwards, until at least the beginning of World War I, articles and works about Hermes Trismegistus and the *Corpus Hermeticum* proliferated, principally in the journals more or less connected with the Theosophical Society, and secondarily in "Rosicrucian" publications:

The Theological and Philosophical Works of Hermes Trismegistus, Christian Neo-Platonist. Translation, preface, and annotations by John David Chambers (Edinburgh, 1882; reissued Ann Arbor, 1967, and New York, 1975).

Reissue of Everard's 1650 edition (London: Redway, 1884), with an Introduction by Hargrave Jennings.

Another reissue of Everard's translation in *Journal of Speculative Philosophy*, vol. XX (1885–1886).

The Hermetic Works; the Virgin of the World of Hermes Mercurius Trismegistus. Now first rendered into English with essay, introduction and notes by Anna Kingsford and E. Maitland. (London: Redway, 1885; reissued Minneapolis, 1977).

The excerpts from Stobaeus (xii–xvii) entitled "The Teachings of Hermes to Ammon," *Corpus Hermeticum* XVI and XVII, and the entirety of the *Asclepius* and of the *Kore Kosmou* were published in English in *The Occult Magazine* (Glasgow), during 1885 and 1886. The identity of the translator is not known, but the version of the *Kore Kosmou* differs from that of Kingsford and Maitland.

Reissue of Everard's 1650 edition, with an introduction by the editor (W. Wynn Westcott): *The Pymander of Hermes*, vol. II of the series "Collectanea Hermetica" (London: Theosophical Publishing Society, 1894).

5. Tradition and Erudition in the Twentieth Century

5A. Persistence of esoteric and hermeneutical exegesis:

Thrice Greatest Hermes: Studies in Hellenistic Theosophy and Gnosis, with commentaries and notes by G. R. S. Mead, 3 vols. (London and Benares: Theosophical Society, 1906; reissued 1964).

German version, Leipzig, 1909.

A. S. Raleigh, *Philosophia Hermetica: A Course of Ten Lessons, Being an Introduction to the "Philosophy of Alchemy"* (San Francisco: Hermetic Publishing Company, 1916).

————. *The Shepherd of Men: An Official Commentary on the Sermon of Hermes Trismegistos* (San Francisco: Hermetic Publishing Company, 1916).

"Hermes Mercurius Trismegistus: A Treatise Preliminary to the Study of Hermetic Philosophy," by Fr. K. X [0], Copyrighted by Societas Rosicruciana in America), Vol. V, May and June 1920 (Nr. 10–11).

The Divine Pymander of Hermes Trismegistus: An Endeavour to Systematize and Elucidate the Corpus Hermeticum. Commentary on the Corpus Hermeticum by the Editors of the Shrine of Wisdom (London, 1923 and various reissues).

Manly Palmer Hall, *An Encyclopedic Outline of Masonic, Hermetic, Qabbalistic and Rosicrucian Philosophy* (Los Angeles: Philosophical Research Society, 1928; reissued 1975, 1979), which contains developments on Hermes Trismegistus and the *Corpus Hermeticum.*

The Gospel of Hermes, new English translation with commentaries by Duncan Greenless (Madras, Theosophical Society, 1949).

Gerard Van Moorsel, *The Mysteries of Hermes Trismegistus, a phenomenologic study in the process of spiritualization in the Corpus Hermeticum and Latin Asclepius* (Utrecht, 1955).

J. Rijckenborgh, *De Egyptische oer-gnosis en haar roop in het eeuwige n'u [. . .] Aan de hand van de Tabula Smaragdina en het Corpus Hermeticum* (Haarlem, 1960–1965).

Lietaert M. Peerbolte, *Poimandres, Grieks-hermetisch geschrift in het Nederlands vertaald met een transpersonalistische beschouwing* (Deventer: Ankh-Hermes bv, 1974).

Robert A. Segal, *The Poimandres as Myth (Scholarly Theory and Gnostic Meaning)* (Berlin: Mouton de Gruyter, 1986).

5B. The *Corpus Hermeticum* and academic study

Real academic study of the *Corpus Hermeticum* begins with Richard Reitzenstein, the first to undertake the study of these texts with full scientific rigor (*Poimandres*, Leipzig, 1904). But naturally one should not underestimate some of his predecessors, such as Casaubon, Tiedemann, Ménard, Pietschmann, nor even Mead (see above for all of these). Esotericism at the end of the nineteenth and beginning of the twentieth century helped to stimulate erudite research into Hermetism. After Reizenstein, text-criticism and erudition are represented above all by Walter Scott and A. J. Festugière:

Hermetica: The ancient Greek and Latin writings which contain religious or philosophic teachings ascribed to Hermes Trismegistus, edited with English translation and notes by Walter Scott, 4 vols. (Oxford, Clarendon Press, 1924–1936; reissued Boston: Shambhala, 1983–1985). Vol. I (1924): Introduction, texts and translation; Vol. II (1925): Notes on the *Corpus Hermeticum;* Vol. III (1926): Notes on the Latin *Asclepius* and the Hermetic extracts of Stobaeus; Vol. IV (1936): *Testimonia,* with introduction, addenda, and indices by A. S. Ferguson. This monumental work is far from being obsolete. Vol. IV, in particular, remains an unsurpassed study of the *Testimonia* (references to the Hermetica in non-Hermetic sources). A compendium of this edition was published in one volume with a foreword by A. G. Gilbert (Bath: Solos Press, 1992).

Poïmandres. Traités II–XVII (du Corpus Hermeticum). Asclepius. Fragments extraits de Stobée, texts established and translated by A. D. Nock and André-Jean Festugière, 4 vols. (Paris: Les Belles Lettres, 1954–1960).

A.-J. Festugière, *La Révélation d'Hermès Trismégiste,* 4 vols. (Paris, 1949-1954; reissued by Les Belles Lettres, 1981).

A.-J. Festugière, *Hermétisme et mystique païenne* (Paris: Aubier-Montaigne, 1967).

The above works of Father Festugière constitute the indispensable basis for scholars. Other studies have appeared, also bearing on the Hermetica properly so-called. There is no question here of

listing all these scholarly works. For that, one can usefully consult
the bibliography presented by A. G. Blanco, cited below, 6B. Let us
cite, though, three important publications: Jean-Pierre Mahé,
Hermès en haute-Egypte: Tome I, *Les textes hermétiques de Nag
Hammadi et leurs parallèles Grecs et Latins*; Tome II, *Le Fragment
du Discours parfait et les Définitions Hermétiques arméniennes*
(Québec: Presses de l'Université Laval, 1978/82). Garth Fowden,
*The Egyptian Hermes: A Historical Approach to the Late Pagan
Mind* (Cambridge University Press, 1986). Brian Copenhaver,
*Hermetica: The Greek Corpus Hermeticum and the Latin Asclepius
in a New English Translation with Notes and Introduction* (Cam-
bridge University Press, 1992).

The next section lists most of the significant studies of the
reception of Alexandrian Hermetism.

6. Studies of the Reception of
Alexandrian Hermetism

6A. Books

Françoise Bonardel, *L'Hermétisme* (Paris: P. U. F., 1985; Series
"Que sais-je?"). A good introduction to Western esotericism in
general, and to the *Corpus Hermeticum* in particular.

Douglas Brooks-Davies, *The Mercurian Monarch: Magical Politics from Spencer to Pope* (Manchester University Press, 1983).

*Christ, Plato, Hermes Trismegistus. The Dawn of Printing.
Catalogue of the Incunabula in the Bibliotheca Philosophica
Hermetica*, 2 vols. Catalogued by Margaret Lane Ford, presented by
M. L. Ford and Frans A. Janssen (Amsterdam: In de Pelikan, 1990);
series "Texts and Studies published by the Bibliotheca Philosophica
Hermetica," no.1.

Brian P. Copenhaver, *Symphorien Champier and the Reception
of the Occultist Tradition in Renaissance France* (The Hague:
Mouton, 1978).

Eugenio Garin, *Medioevo e Rinascimento*, Bari, 1954.

―――, *La cultura filosofica del Rinascimento italiano*, Florence, 1961.

————, *Ermetismo del Rinascimento*, Rome: Editori Riuniti, Biblioteca minima, 1988.

Jeanne Ellen Harrie, *François Foix de Candale and the Hermetic Tradition in XVIth century France*, Ph.D. diss., University of California, Riverside, 1975.

Hermes Trismegistus Pater Philosophorum (Tekstgeschiedenis van het Corpus Hermeticum), Exhibition in the Bibliotheca Philosophica Hermetica, Amsterdam, 1990. Presented by Joseph R. Ritman, Frans B. Janssen, and F. Van Lamoen.

Hermeticism in the Renaissance. Intellectual History and the Occult in early modern Europe, ed. Ingrid Merkel and Allen G. Debus (Washington: Folger Books; London and Toronto: Associated University Presses, 1988); Symposium held in March, 1982, at the Folger Shakespeare Library, Washington, D.C. See Section 6B, below, for most articles from this collective work.

Henry and Renée Kahane, *The Krater and the Grail. Hermetic sources of the Parzival* (Urbana: University of Illinois Press, 1965; Illinois Studies in Language and Literature, vol. LVI).

P. O. Kristeller, *Studies in Renaissance Thought and Letters* (Rome, 1966).

Mercure à la Renaissance. Collective work presented by M. M. de La Garanderie. Proceedings of the Conference of Lille, 1984. (Paris: H. Hampion, 1988). For titles of some of the contributions relevant to our subject, see infra, 6B.

Claudio Moreschini, *Dall'Asclepius al Crater Hermetis. Studi sull'ermetismo latino-tardo-antico e renascimentale* (Pisa, 1985).

Luminita Irene Niculescu, "From Hermeticism to Hermeneutics: Alchemical Metaphors in Renaissance Literature," Ph.D. diss., University of California, Los Angeles, 1981.

Présence d'Hermès Trismégiste, ed. Antoine Faivre (Paris: Albin Michel, 1988; collection "Cahiers de l'Hermétisme") See Section 6B, below, for some articles from this collective work.

Gennaro Savarese, *La cultura a Roma tra unaenesimo e ermetismo (1480–1540)* (Rome: De Rubeis, 1993).

Robert Schuler, *English Magical Poems* (New York: Garland, 1979).

Wayne Shumaker, *The Occult Sciences in the Renaissance: A Study in Intellectual Patterns* (Berkeley: University of California Press, 1972. Reprint, 1979). See chapter *Hermes Trismegistus*, pp.201–251.

Mirko Sladek, *Fragmente der hermetischen Philosophie in der Naturphilosophie der Neuzeit* (Berne: Peter Lang, Publications universitaires européennes, 1984); French translation: *L'Etoile d'Hermès* (Paris: Albin Michel, 1992). On the *Corpus Hermeticum* and the forms it took with Giordano Bruno, Henry More, Thomas Vaughan, Goethe.

Testi umanistici su l'Ermetismo (Rome: Fratelli Boca, Archivio de Filosofia, 1955). Collective work, with very important articles on Lazarelli, Giorgi, Agrippa. See section 6B, below, under Brini, Vasoli, Zambelli.

Ernest Lee Tuveson, *The Avatars of Thrice Great Hermes: An Approach to Romanticism* (Lewisburg: Bucknell University Press, 1982). On the philosophy of the *Corpus Hermeticum* and the forms it took in the Romantic era, especially in Anglo-Saxon countries.

D. P. Walker, *The Ancient Theology: Studies in Christian Platonism from the Fifteenth to the Eighteenth Century* (London: Duckworth, 1972).

———, *Spiritual and Demonic Magic from Ficino to Campanella* (London: Warburg Institute, 1958; reissued 1969, 1975); French translation, *La magie spirituelle et angélique, de Ficin à Campanella* (Paris: Albin Michel, 1988).

Robert Westman and J. E. McGuire, *Hermeticism and the Scientific Revolution* (Los Angeles: William Andrews Clark Memorial Library, University of California, 1977).

Frances A. Yates, *Giordano Bruno and the Hermetic Tradition* (London: Routledge & Kegan Paul, 1964). Although now disputed on several points, this book remains a masterpiece and an indispensable resource. French translation, *Giordano Bruno et la tradition hermétique* (Paris: Dervy, 1988).

6B. Articles (a selection, not an exhaustive list):

Michael Allen, "Marsile Ficin, Hermès et le Corpus Hermeticum," in *Présence d'Hermès Trismégiste* (see 6A, above), pp.110–119.

Antonio Gonzalez Blanco, "Hermetism: A Bibliographical Approach," in *Aufstieg und Niedergang der römischen Welt (Geschichte und Kultur Roms im Spiegel der neuren Forschung)*, vol. II (4. Teilband: *Religion*), ed. W. Haase (Berlin/New York: Walter de Gruyter, 1984), pp.2240–2281.

Mirella Brini, "Ludovico Lazarelli: Epistola Enoch, Dal Crater Hermetis, Vade Mecum," in *Testi umanistici* (see 6A, above), pp.21–27.

Brian Copenhaver, "Hermes Trismegistus, Proclus, and the Problem of a Philosophy of Magic in the Renaissance," in *Hermeticism in the Renaissance* (see 6A, above), pp.79–110.

Jean Dagens, "Le Commentaire du Pimandre de Foix de Candale," in *Mélanges d'histoire littéraire offerts à Daniel Mornet* (Paris: Nizet, 1951), pp.21–26.

——, "Hermétisme et Cabale en France de Lefèvre d'Etaples à Bossuet," in *Revue de littérature comparée*, no. 1 (1961), pp.5–16.

K. H. Dannenfeldt, Marie-Thérèse d'Alverny, and Théodore Silverstein, "Hermetica Philosophica" and "Oracula Chaldaica," in *Catalogus Translationum et Commentariorum: Medieval and Renaissance Latin Translations and Commentaries. Annotated lists and guides*, ed. Paul Oskar Kristeller, Vols. 1–2 (Washington, DC: Catholic University of America Press, 1960). This catalogue is an indispensable research tool.

B. J. T. Dobbs, "Newton's *Commentary* on the *Emerald Tablet* of Hermes Trismegistus: Its Scientific and Theological Significance," in *Hermeticism in the Renaissance* (see 6A, above), pp.182–191.

Harrie Jeanne Ellen, "Duplessis-Mornay, Foix de Candale and the Hermetic Religion of the World," in *Renaissance Quarterly*, vol. 31 (1978), pp.499–514.

Antoine Faivre, "Hermetism," in Mircea Eliade, ed., *The Encyclopedia of Religion* (New York: Macmillan, 1987), vol. VI, pp.293–

302. General panorama of the reception of Alexandrian Hermetism in Europe.

David R. Fideler, "The Path Toward the Grail: The Hermetic Sources and Structure of Wolfram von Eschenbach's *Parzival*," in *Alexandria: The Journal of the Western Cosmological Traditions* 1 (Grand Rapids: Phanes Press, 1991), pp. 187–227.

Gianfranco Formichetti, "Ermete Trismegisto nelle opere di Tommaso Campanella," in *La città dei segreti: Magia, astrologia e cultura esoterica a Roma (XV–XVIII sec.)*, ed. Fabio Torelli. Milan: Franco Angeli Libri, 1985); Symposium "Roma Ermetica," Rome, October, 1983.

Eugenio Garin, "Nota sull'ermetismo," in *La Cultura Philosophica del Rinascimento Italiano* (Florence: Sansoni, 1961), pp.143–165.

J. S. Gill, "How Hermes Trismegistus was introduced to Renaissance England: the influences of Caxton and Ficino's *Argumentum* on Baldwin and Palfreyman," in *Journal of the Warburg and Courtauld Institutes*, vol. 47 (1984), pp.222–225.

Anthony Thomas Grafton, "Protestant versus Prophet: Isaac Casaubon on Hermes Trismegistus," in *Journal of the Warburg and Courtauld Institutes*, vol. 46 (1983), pp.78–93.

Moshe Idel, "Hermeticism and Judaism," in *Hermeticism in the Renaissance* (see 6A, above), pp.59–76.

Frans A. Janssen, "Dutch Translations of the *Corpus Hermeticum*," in *Theatrum orbis librorum* (Liber amicorum Nico Israel) (Utrecht, 1989), pp. 230–241.

Karin Johannison, "Magic, Science, and Institutionalization in the 17th and 18th centuries," in *Hermeticism in the Renaissance* (see 6A, above), pp.151–162.

Henry and Renée Kahane, "Hermetism in the Alfonsine Tradition," in *Mélanges offerts à Rita Lejeune* (Gembloux: Éditions J. Duculot, 1969), vol. I, pp.443–457.

Paul Oskar Kristeller, "Lodovico Lazarelli e Giovanni da Corregio: due ermetici del Quattrocento. Manoscritto II.D.I.4. della Biblioteca Communale degli Ardenti della Città di Viterbo," in *Studi e*

Richerche nel 1500 della fondazione Viterbe (Agnesotti, 1961), pp.3–25.

———, "Marsilio Ficino e Lodovico Lazarelli. Contributo alla diffusione delle idee ermetiche nel Rinascimento," in *Annali della R. Scuola Normale Superiore di Pisa (Lettere, Storia e Filosofia)* (Bologna: N. Zanichelli, 1938), series II, vol. VII, pp.237–262.

Pierre Lory, "Hermes/Idris, prophète et sage de la tradition islamique," in *Présence d'Hermès Trismègiste* (see 6A, above), pp.100–109.

Jean-Françoise Maillard, "Hermès théologien et philosophe," in *Mercure à la Renaissance* (see 6A, above), pp. 11–14.

———, "Mercure alchimiste dans la tradition mytho-hermétique," in *ibid.*, pp. 117–130.

Isabelle Pantin, "Les commentaires de Lefèvre d'Etaples au *Corpus Hermeticum*," in *Présence d'Hermès Trismégiste* (see 6A, above), pp.167–183).

Martin Plessner, "Hermes Trismegistus and Arab Science," in *Studia Islamica*, vol. II (1954), pp.45–59.

F. Purnell, "Hermes and the Sybil: A Note on Ficino's Pimander," in *Renaissance Quarterly*, vol. 30 (1977), pp.305–310.

———, "Francesco Patrizi and the Critics of Hermes Trismegistus," in *Journal of Medieval and Renaissance Studies*, vol. 6 (1976), pp.155–178.

Julius Ruska, "Studien zu Muhammad Ibn Umail," in *Isis. Quarterly Organ of the History of Science Society*, vol. XXIV/1 (Dec. 1935), pp.310–342.

Charles B. Schmitt, "Perennial Philosophy: From Agostino Steuco to Leibniz," in *Journal of the History of Ideas*, vol. 27 (Jan.–March 1966), pp.505–532.

———, "Prisca Theologia e Philosophia perennis: due temi del Rinascimento italiano e la loro fortuna," in *Atti del V Convegno internazionale del Centro di Studi Umanistici: Il pensiero italiano del Rinascimento e il tempo nostro* (Florence: Olschki, 1970), pp.211–236.

Wayne Shumaker, "Literary Hermeticism: Some Test Cases," in

Hermeticism in the Renaissance (see 6A, above), pp.293–301.

Théodore Silverstein, "Liber Hermetis Mercurii Triplicis de VI Rerum Principiis," in *Archives d'histoire doctrinale et littéraire du Moyen Age* (Paris: Vrin, 1956), yr. 1955, pp.217–302.

————, "The Fabulous Cosmogony of Bernardus Silvester," in *Modern Philology* XLVI (1948), pp.92–116.

Mirko Sladek, "Mercurius Triplex, Mercurius Termaximus et les 'trois Hermès'," in *Présence d'Hermès Trismégiste* (see 6A, above), pp.88–99.

Loris Sturlese, "Saints et Magiciens: Albert le Grand en face d'Hermès Trismégiste," in *Archives de philosophie*, vol. 43 (1980), pp.615–634.

Robert Jan Van Pelt, "The Utopian Exit of the Hermetic Temple: or a Curious Transition in the Tradition of the Cosmic Sanctuary," in *Hermeticism in the Renaissance* (see 6A, above), pp.400–423.

Cesare Vasoli, "Ermetismo e cabala nel tardo Rinascimento e nel primo '600," in *La città dei segreti* (see above, under Formichetti), pp.103–108.

————, "Francesco Giorgio Veneto," in *Testi umanistici* (see 6A, above), pp. 79–104.

————, "Temi e fonti della tradizione ermetica in uno scritto di Symphorien Champier," in *Umanesimo e esoterismo*, a collective work edited by Enrico Castelli (Padova: Cedam, 1960), pp.235–289.

————, "Mercure dans la tradition ficinienne," in *Mercure à la Renaissance* (see 6A above), pp.27–43.

————, "L'Hermétisme à Venise, de Giorgio à Patrizi," in *Présence d'Hermès Trismégiste* (see 6A, above), pp.120–152.

————, "L'Hermétisme dans l'*Oraculum* de Giovanni Nesi," in *Présence d'Hermès Trismégiste* (see 6A, above), pp.153–156.

Frances A. Yates, "The Hermetic Tradition in Renaissance Science," in *Art, Science and History in the Renaissance* (Baltimore: C. S. Singleton, 1968), pp.155–274.

Paola Zambelli, "Cornelius Agrippa di Nettesheim," in *Testi umanistici* (see 6A, above), pp.105–162.

————, "Scholastic and Humanist Views of Hermeticism and

Witchcraft," in *Hermeticism in the Renaissance* (see 6A, above), pp.125–153.

Index of Names

PHANES PRESS publishes quality books on philosophy, mythology, ancient religions, the humanities, cosmology, and culture. To receive a copy of our catalogue, write:

Phanes Press
PO Box 6114
Grand Rapids, MI 49516
USA

www.phanes.com